T0146932

Is the
Devil Allergic
to Shrubbery?

UNDERSTANDING THE HEDGE OF PROTECTION

JEFF TUCK

WESTBOW
PRESS®
A DIVISION OF THOMAS NELSON
& ZONDERVAN

WestBow Press books may be ordered through booksellers or by contacting:

WestBow Press
A Division of Thomas Nelson & Zondervan
1663 Liberty Drive
Bloomington, IN 47403
www.westbowpress.com
844-714-3454

Scripture quotations are taken from the Holy Bible, New International Version®, NIV®. Copyright © 1973, 1978, 1984 by Biblica, Inc.™ Used by permission of Zondervan. All rights reserved worldwide.

ISBN: 979-8-3850-0745-5 (sc)
ISBN: 979-8-3850-0746-2 (hc)
ISBN: 979-8-3850-0747-9 (e)

Library of Congress Control Number: 2023917596

Print information available on the last page.

WestBow Press rev. date: 09/18/2023

Introduction

The Hedge of Protection

Years ago, I was watching the Christian comedian Tim Hawkins. This is not a plug for you to watch him, but this is a plug for you to watch him (Tim, feel free to sponsor my book if you ever read this). Tim Hawkins is hilarious. While I have gotten a ton of laughs from him, I have also been challenged to think by his sketches. For those of you that know Tim Hawkins' work, you are probably a little nervous at this point. I mean, who draws inspiration from a comedian?

I promise you, this is a serious Biblical study. I felt the call to write this book when I was going through a particularly difficult situation in my life. I needed God's protection and His intervention. I was suffering anxiety attacks every day, so I went to comedy for some modicum of relief. This is when I rewatched the Tim Hawkins sketch. Tim is reacting to a common phrase in Christian circles- I'm praying a hedge of protection around you. Tim's response is classic:

> **I don't mean to complain, but is that the best you can do? How about a thick cement wall? With razor wire on top of that bad boy. A Hedge of Protection? A good set of clippers would get right through that. I bet the devil has a set of clippers.**

I got a good laugh out of his comment, but then I really began to think about God's protection.

This wondering led me to investigate God's Hedge of Protection, and I found out that it does not exist. God's protection exists, and God's hedge exists. The Hedge of Protection does not exist. The Book of Job is the closest mention of the Hedge of Protection.

> **One day the angels came to present themselves before the LORD, and Satan also came with them. The LORD said to Satan, "Where have you come from?" Satan answered the LORD, "From roaming throughout the earth, going back and forth on it." Then the LORD said to Satan, "Have you considered my servant Job? There is no one on earth like him; he is blameless and upright, a man who fears God and shuns evil." Does Job fear God for nothing?" Satan replied. "Have you not put a hedge around him and his household and everything he has? You have blessed the work of his hands, so that his flocks and herds are spread throughout the land. But now stretch out your hand and strike everything he has, and he will surely curse you to your face." The LORD said to Satan, "Very well, then, everything he has is in your power, but on the man himself do not lay a finger." Job 1: 6-12**

A look at these verses shows that God definitely puts a Hedge around us. The devil wanted a piece of Job, but God prevented the devil with a Hedge. We automatically assume that the Hedge was one of protection, but this assumption cheapens what the Hedge does.

The devil states that God's Hedge was one of blessing. Paul tells us that:

> **For I am convinced that neither death nor life, neither angels nor demons, neither the present nor the future, nor any powers, neither height nor depth, nor anything else in all creation, will be able to separate us from the love of God that is in Christ Jesus our Lord. Romans 8:38-39**

Our blessing comes from God's love for us, and nothing can impact His love for us. In I John 4:16, we are told that God is love. We can easily see that the Hedge is made up of God Himself, intervening on our behalf. Now, this intervention is one of blessing and one of protection, so the idea of a Hedge of Protection is not wrong or heresy. The Hedge is just so much more than protection.

Once I realized that the Hedge was more than just protection, I started looking into hedges and hedgerows. The hedge/hedgerow is useful in many ways. It protects the inside of the hedge from being invaded by unwanted animals. It also provides shade, which prevents scorching and evaporation. I will discuss several uses of the hedge in this book, but every use comes back to one idea: the hedge allows growth. In a gardening sense, hedges allow crops to grow; in a spiritual sense, hedges allow our faith to grow.

In order for a hedge to be effective, it has to keep out many different invaders. Anyone who gardens knows that small animals like rabbits can easily go under a fence, and animals like deer can jump a fence. A good hedge consists of many different types of foliage. The hedge should have tall trees or shrubs that are too tall to jump over; it should also have shrubs that are dense and close to the ground to prevent mice and rabbits from going through. A good root system can help discourage burrowing animals as well. A denser hedge means more safety- just like a deeper faith means safety in trouble.

The interesting thing about Hedges is that they protect growth as they grow. The Hedge is a living, growing entity. Our faith is a living, growing entity. Seeing your faith as an entity is a little weird, but our faith is a belief in something outside of our natural, physical existence. The philosophers call us finite and God infinite. We have the infinite Holy Spirit inside us. We are by nature not holy, so the holiness must be something foreign coming into us. Our Hedge protects growth, but growth of what? Our infinite faith. Our faith is a growing, or shrinking, faith. Faith and growth are so inextricably linked that they must be handled together. Our Hedge protects, promotes, and assures both.

My study of the Hedge is going to be broken into three sections: what it is, what goes on behind the Hedge, and what it is not. I have included some questions for you to consider as you go. Hopefully, this will help you as much as it helped me. My prayer is that your faith will grow and that your Hedge will become a multi-tiered defense that leaves you with a Job like faith.

PART I

What does the Hedge Do?

The Hedge as Protection

When I was young, I was a huge collector of stuffed animals. One of the oldest members of my collection was a frog I called Ribbie. My mom gave me Ribbie when I was about three years old. When I was ten, my mom died a couple of months before Christmas, but she had already purchased a new member to my collection: a holiday Garfield stuffed animal holding a candy cane and sporting a candy cane striped sleeping hat. My mom lost her life in a horrific way that forced me to learn a lesson about life: the things that you read about in the papers or see in the movies actually happen to real people. I learned that lesson and became terrified of ever experiencing hardship again. Nighttime and darkness were very trying times for me, so I ran to something to make me feel safe: Ribbie and Garfield.

Running for safety to a couple of plush figures wasn't wrong, but it wasn't really going to give me anything other than imaginary protection. It did provide me with the comfort that my mom was still with me in memory, and I had something physical to hold and to cry on. Honestly, Ribbie and Garf were more physical reminders of the love that my mom had for me and that the pain that was thrust upon could never steal the love that I felt when I held onto my protectors. Ribbie and Garf were more than just a stuffed animal and more than a physical protection- it had the deeper meaning that the love that my mom and I had for each other was undying. Life often has a deeper meaning than we see at face value.

Thinking of the Hedge as a hedge of protection isn't any more wrong than me holding onto Ribbie when I was scared, but it is short sighted in how much the Hedge can do in our spiritual life. It is interesting that we focus on it as a hedge of protection when that pairing is never made in the Bible. Yes, the Hedge does form a protective barrier for our lives, but it is protective at a far deeper level than what we realize.

What things in your life have a deeper meaning than face value?

What things remind you of a better time?

What do you run to when you have pain and fear?

There is no greater Biblical analogy/parable for the importance of the Hedge than the Parable of the Sower in Luke 8:5 and 11-12 (NIV).

> **A farmer went out to sow his seed. As he was scattering the seed, some fell along the path; it was trampled on, and the birds ate it up ... The seed is the word of God. Those along the path are the ones who hear, and then the devil comes and takes away the word from their hearts, so that they may not believe and be saved.**

A lot of us would draw from this that we need to guard the Word in our heart to keep it from being stolen, and while correct, it is a very basic understanding. Remember, Paul told us that not everyone is ready for spiritual food and that some are stuck in elementary teachings of God. Jesus was explaining the parable in very basic terms- what the disciples were ready for at that moment.

Still, this portion of Scripture has a deeper meaning that we cannot miss. First, the seed was scattered on the path. Why would seed fall on the path? Was the farmer bad at his job and went scattering away from the field? We have to assume that the farmer knew what he was doing since Jesus never condemns the farmer's carelessness. Instead, we have to understand that the farmer was scattering near the edge of the field and that the seed found its way outside of the area where growth can be done. This is key in that the people that were hearing the Word were not where they were supposed to be but had wandered out of the field and ended up in the path (broad is the path that leads to destruction).

Too often, people live their life on the edge of right and wrong. Jesus warned that two masters cannot be served, yet as people we try to have a foot in the church and a foot in the world. This leads us into land that is not productive to growth and safety. The need to stay away from the edges of life cannot be stated more clearly than what happens with the Word of God in a person's life.

The Scripture goes on to tell us that the Word of God (the seed) is trampled. Let's take a second and explore where trampling is used in the Bible. The word trampled is used multiple times in the Bible. The seventh chapter of Micah describes a nation that has completely lost its moral compass and how the most upright are like thorns (something that leaves those who get near with burning wounds). How bad must this country have been where the best are so evil that they wound everyone they contact. Micah promised that these mockers and irreverent people would be judged and a public shamed as God trampled them and exposed their uncleanliness.

Jesus made mention of trampling at the Sermon on the Mount when he talked about the salt. What happened when the salt lost its saltiness? It was trampled on as it was unfit to be used for anything. It was literal rubbish that needed to be disposed of immediately, just as the devil would be trampled in judgment in Romans 16:20. Also, think of the serpent that tricked Adam and Eve and how it would be crushed (trampled) by the heel of man.

Isaiah uses the idea of trampling several times. In 10:6, Isaiah describes a godless nation that will be trampled down in the mud for invoking God's fury. In 63:6, Isaiah tells how the wicked would be trampled down and their life blood poured out on the streets. In 25:10, Moab would be trampled down as straw is stomped into the water of a manure pile. At least to me, trampling sounds like a very bad thing, but Isaiah adds another verse that was one of the earliest verses that I learned, 53:5, when he describes how the Man of Sorrow (Jesus) would be trampled or crushed when he takes on our sins. We know what type of death Jesus took. Is this what a trampling looks like? A death by crucifixion where the person slowly suffocates as their legs give out from strain and the pain of having nerves severed by the railroad sized spikes that go through the feet and the arms?

Looking at trampling as just being walked on completely misses how horrible the loss of the Word and the missed opportunity to bear fruit in the field is. Remember when God said that the Church at Laodicea was lukewarm (ie being on the edge of the field or having one foot in both the world and the church)? If not, read Revelation 3, but for those that do remember, it is important to remember that God said He would vomit out the lukewarm. Those that allowed the word to be trampled in their life brought a desire in God to retch. While I would like to avoid graphic detail, take a minute to really think about what vomiting entails. I hate to vomit: I can't breathe, it hurts, it leaves a bad taste in my mouth, it leads to dry heaving, and it seems like it will never end. I invariably end up hugging a very dirty toilet with tears streaming down my eyes praying that this feeling will end quickly. Those living on the fringe of faith invoke such an emotion and a reaction.

Going back to the parable, the birds of the air would come in and gobble up the seeds. Again, this has a far more vivid imagery that we realize. We need to look at where animals have been used in judgment in the Bible. In 1 Kings 13, a prophet is sent out to Israel to condemn it for its idol worship and for turning away from the true God. The prophet is given specific instructions to not stop in Israel nor to not take food from its inhabitants; unfortunately, a man tricks the prophet into having dinner at his house. On the way home, the prophet is killed by a lion and his body left on the road.

In the Pentateuch, Joshua and Exodus both tell a story about the Lord sending hornets to drive out the inhabitants of Canaan so that the Israelites could have their Promised Land. In Exodus, the people grumbled against the Lord about how they detested Manna and did not have enough water. Take a second to think how amazing Manna was and how great the gift of it was to the people. Also remember that Moses brought water out of a rock for the people. This was a direct challenge to God's miraculous works. The result was poisonous snakes killing those that complained. We could go on to talk about the Plagues of Frogs, Insects, and the like that God used to punish Pharaoh for his disobedience.

Still the greatest story of animal justice has to be the story of Elisha and the Two Bears. This is one of the most misunderstood stories in the Bible. In 2 Kings 2, Elisha calls down a curse on a group of "boys", and two bears immediately maul over 40 people. First, let's really unpack what youth means (go to 1517 Org[1] and look up the explanation if you want the Hebrew words). The phrase used for small boys was used by Solomon when he took over as king in his 20s. It can also be used for servant or priest. It is also important to

---

[1]   Bird, Chad. (February, 2020). 1517. *The Misunderstood Story of Bear Attacks, Bald Prophets, and Forty-two Mouthy "Kids"*. https://www.1517. org/articles/the-misunderstood-story-of-bear-attacks-a-bald-prophet-and-forty-two-mouthy-kids

remember that this event took place at Bethel, which was one of the two places of idol worship that Jeroboam had set up to keep Israel from worshiping God in Jerusalem. It is very likely that these "boys" were actually pagan priests that stood in direct opposition to the God of Abraham. It is even easier to see how bad the behavior was when we see the taunts of these priests. Elisha was called baldhead. In Biblical times, baldness was often associated with skin diseases, which were often lumped together under the term leprosy. Lepers and those suffering from skin maladies were often considered unclean and unfit for religious worship. The second thing of note is that priests said, "Go up, Go up". What a weird thing to say, right? No, they were referencing how Elisha's master, the prophet Elijah, was taken up to Heaven in a chariot of fire. In essence, this large group of priests were saying something akin to "why don't you just die or leave the Earth" and were mocking the miraculous work of God taking a righteous man to Heaven without his experiencing death.

The attack and mauling of this group was a divine punishment for extreme disrespect to miracles, God's chosen people, and God's power/authority. In each case, animals were used for judgment in situations that were so despicable and vile that normal punishment or methods of making a point were no longer enough. The real purpose of this part of the parable is to paint a picture of people that have so angered God by their inability to respect the authority of God that they must be vomited out or utterly destroyed.

How this applies to the Hedge is that the Hedge protects us from this being our fate. You see, a Hedge does multiple things. First, it serves a boundary that we do not cross. I grew up in a Holiness Movement church which stressed boundaries. These weren't just normal boundaries, but the focus was to set the boundary so far away from the line where the field ends and path begins that there is no hope that the seeds would fall onto infertile ground. Boundaries are protective and beautiful as they keep you from divine punishment.

Where are those boundaries? It is different for each person and requires God to show you what you're ready for in your life. It is also custom made for what you personally struggle with in your life. What is it that can take you too close to the edge? Those are where you need the thickest and densest Hedge to keep you from straying onto a bad path.

<u>What boundaries do you need in your life?</u>

<u>Are there areas where you struggle to want to put boundaries?</u>

The Biblical Archeology Society[2] humorously states that reading the Jungle Book would introduce you to the animals that the Biblical Jews had to confront. Lions, tigers, hippos, crocodiles, snakes, boars, leopards, bears, panthers, cheetahs, and hundreds of other dangerous animals were a constant threat to a farming community or those traveling on the road between towns. It isn't always even the dangerous animals that are a threat. Everyone who has ever tried to raise a garden has stories of critters that nibble away on the lettuce or bugs that decimate the tomatoes. The spiritual analogy is that life has a lot of different methods of pulling your astray and eating the seeds that are planted in your heart.

The Hedge is a boundary not just for you, but it is also a boundary for your temptations. Remember, the Hedge is best when it is five to ten feet thick and made up of several different types of plant (small and large shrubs, trees, flowers, etc). Your spiritual hedge must be a multi-tiered defense against temptation as you will face many in your life. We live in a society where alcohol is prevalent, and I know that I have the predisposition to be an abuser of substances. Part of my Hedge is that I don't spend time around alcohol or even have the

---

2   Slifkin, nRabbi Dr. Natan. (March, 2022). The Biblical Archeology Society. *Bible Animals: From Hyenas to Hippos*. <u>https://www.biblicalarchaeology.org/daily/biblical-topics/hebrew-bible/bible-animals/</u>

occasional social drink. I hold very firmly to the strict boundary of Paul's "it might be permissible but is it beneficial". Everything that is not beneficial must be kept out of my field, or my field becomes an infertile path too quickly. When I was in my pre-Christ days, I grew up in area that used, as I did, a ton of profanity. I have since removed those words from my jargon, but I have gone further by removing R Rated movies and MA rated TV shows because they could possibly put those words back in my mind. This is done to help build another layer of hedge to keep the path away from my field.

<u>What are the areas that you know are a temptation in your life? Is it things, feelings, people, or something else?</u>

<u>What things do you need to add into your Hedge to protect you from temptations?</u>

Finally, the Hedge protects our seed from being trampled from outside forces. A strong hedge keeps out dangerous animals, other people, and anything else that could unearth your seeds. The Hedge is that barrier that bars entry to everything that does not belong in your life and anything that can steal away your joy. Remember, the Word of God is the most precious thing in the world. In John 1, Jesus was called the Word, and the Bible is the Word. Let this sink in, your Hedge is constructed from the Word: Jesus and the Bible. How can you stand up against temptation unless Jesus is in your heart and the Bible is in your mind. This combination is an unbeatable, unassailable fortress. Growing up, I fell in love with the word bastion. Don't ask me why. I was a weird child that liked the thesaurus and dictionary. The word bastion has two main meanings, according to pretty much every dictionary known to man: a part of a fortification that allows defensive fire from several directions or a person who strongly upholds a principle. Your Hedge must be a bastion: a mixture of you strongly upholding your faith and of you defensively taking down all attacks on your faith- and you must do it from several directions.

What area of your walk or faith needs to be more strongly upheld in your life?

What area of your walk or faith is not being defended from several directions?

What changes do you need to make in your life to help you from being lukewarm?

Hedge of False Beliefs

I came across a research study awhile back that said that humans take the loss of a pet harder than the loss of most family members. It's odd how these furry little creatures can wiggle into our hearts; still, it is even more peculiar to me that people can go the opposite direction: animal abuse. I came across a story a few years back about a rescued dog: a big German Shepherd that had been abused. I applauded this person for trying to rehabilitate the dog, but like humans, the emotional scars on animals don't always heal. Unfortunately, the rescuer found out that good intentions and naivety do not create favorable results. Having faith in the wrong thing can have disastrous consequences.

The Parable of the Sower illustrates that birds come and steal away what God is trying to plant into our hearts. It is interesting to note that Jesus describes people losing what God is trying to plant this way:

> **A farmer went out to sow his seed. As he was scattering the seed, some fell along the path, and the birds came and ate it up. When anyone hears the message about the kingdom and does not understand it, the evil one comes and snatches away what was sown in their heart. This is the seed sown along the path. Matthew 13:3-4, 19**

Notice that Jesus states that we lose our growing opportunity because we don't understand the message.

It is easy to write about this lack of understanding to deep spiritual truths; unfortunately, too many people get lost in the basics. Remember, the Bible calls Jesus the cornerstone in Ephesians 2:20. You might not be much into building, but the cornerstone is the first stone laid in a foundation. In essence, the entire building is constructed around this one stone. In construction, the cornerstone sets the stability and the direction of the building; in faith terms, the cornerstone is the foundation of our faith and sets the direction of where our belief is to go. Yet, Jesus states in Matthew 21:42 that the religious leaders (those that were supposedly super educated and godly) would reject the cornerstone.

The rejection of the cornerstone is important for two reasons. First, it means that the religious or the "god followers" were rejecting the very basis of the faith. Second, the rejection of Jesus was done because of a lack of knowledge of the Word. This seems trivial, but an understanding of Jewish culture opens up a new understanding. Jewish education could range from a memorization of the first five books of the Old Testament to the advanced memorization of all of the Old Testament. The religious leaders that "did not understand" the Scriptures were people that had memorized the entire Old Testament. This is not a misunderstanding of new believers who do not understand God, though it does apply to them; the misunderstanding is because the recipients of God's Word had chosen to misinterpret the truth- the cornerstone was rejected.

When Jesus was tempted in the wilderness, the enemy used twisted Scripture and wrong understandings to lure Jesus away. Getting people to misrepresent and misunderstand the Bible is the enemy's best weapon. We as Christians must be carefully guarding our minds as we read Scripture: as Paul states, test every spirit. We have to test every spirit, every thought, and every belief because this is what protects us from the enemy or opens us up to the enemy.

The enemy is still working to mislead us, and he starts off by getting us to misunderstand Creation. While animals as creators are rare, several ethnic groups make use of animals in their creation stories. Granted, the Bible also mentions animals in our Creation story, but there are differences. The Bible mentions God creating animals and the Serpent misleading Eve, thereby causing the Fall. The Biblical use of animals is markedly different from the aforementioned uses. These other groups use the animals as creators. A prime example is the Indigenous peoples of North America that believe the world was made on the back of a turtle, with animals going into the deep waters to find dirt to put on the turtle's back. Some African tribes believe that the world is held up by a giant serpent. These myths, and others, should be heretical to Christians because it takes the Creation away from Creator God.

Another theft of intellectual property by animals is the fixation that scientists have with evolution. The idea that we came from animals is not just a science phenomenon as some early Chinese tribes believed that they descended from a dog deity, Indigenous North Americans believe that man came from bears in some way, and one of the main Egyptian creation stories has a cosmic egg being made by a group of amphibians (frogs and snakes). The premise of evolution is solidly rooted in the belief that there was no man until we changed from an animal: single cells transformed into different multicellular organisms that transform into different sea creatures that become other creatures that eventually become humans and all of the animals that we have today.

Belief in evolution is heresy and sin. Animals did not become man- God created man. The Bible says that God formed man from the dust, whereas God spoke animals into existence. There is no correlation between the two in the Bible. Just as there is no evidence of evolution in the Bible, there is no evidence in the real world. This is not the forum for a whole evolution discussion, and there are others that have already done the heavy lifting on this. Lee Stroebel wrote a book called *The Case for Creation* that goes in depth on how the Christian Creation story is the most likely. Michael Behee wrote a book entitled *Darwin's Black Box* where he destroys evolution from a microbiological level. Stroebel is an award-winning journalist that interviews experts in science fields, while Behee is one of the leading microbiologists in the world. These two, along with countless others, firmly establish Creation as a divine work.

Even though there is no evidence of evolution and plenty of evidence pointing to our God's hand in creation, people still fail to grasp what is taught in the first book of the Bible about the first man: God created everything. This is Faith 101 so to speak.

Ye, people want to go astray and espouse animals into worship. And yes, we worship animals. Animal deities are rampant in the world. The Aztec god Huitzilopochtli is a hummingbird; Hinduism has Ganesha, with an elephant head, and Vishnu who takes the form of several animals; Aborigines have a Rainbow snake deity; Celtics have a stag deity; and several other societies follow a similar path.

Egypt was a polytheistic society that was known for animal deities. One of their chief gods was Anubis, who is usually depicted as a human with a dog head or as some sort of dog-like creature. Horus, a man with a bird head, was another one of these important gods. According to Egyptian lore, the god Geb took goose form and laid an egg that would become our world. I could give a list of gods that were animal related that would exhaust you.

Animal worship does not even just take the form of deities but go into general worship. Throughout the world, pigs, snakes, tigers, cattle, elephants, monkeys, wolves, cats, etc are worshiped in some fashion. The elevation of animals into deity is a common part of our world, but it is not Biblical. The Bible tells us that we are formed in God's image, and we do not have the form of an animal. There was a song from Audio Adrenaline called *My God* that speaks to this perfectly in an old remix that is hard to find:

> **Reverend Moody, I believe in a big fat cow**
> **[Rev Moody]: My God died on the Cross, not at**
> **McDonald's**
> **Jesus lives, Jesus lives**

Inclusion of animals into our pantheon or our worship is idol worship- sin. The accuser purposefully is trying to get us to reject a God that created the world, then created man, to then send His Son down in the form of a man to free that man from the snares of the enemy. Our God came to Earth to die on the cross; He did not come down to Earth as an animal that only evolved into a man by happenstance when it could have evolved into a future McDonald's hamburger.

I get it, you probably don't worship a dog headed deity or believe that the world came from a cosmic egg. I don't want you to think that you just wasted your devotional time because my guess is that you have in some way strayed into "animal worship". We have all been misled- for all have sinned and fallen short of the Glory of God.

Do you worship animals? (trick question as I know you will say no, but I am setting you up)

Are there areas in your life where you know that other Christians would disagree with your actions and with your theology?

Would you act the same way, state an opinion, or tell a life story to the pastor/priest that you would the people you work with, hang out with, or meet in the supermarket?

Do you ever trivialize something that the Bible states as something for a different society or time?

Answering yes to these questions is a good indicator that you have "worshiped animals". I admittedly tricked you as sin is a part of everyone's past, so you and I have both fallen into following the wrong entity.

Let's go to Exodus 32 for a moment. The situation is one that was getting out of hand and almost led to God wiping out the Israelites. Moses had gone up to Mt. Horeb to talk to God, and he was gone for quite some time. The Israelites got antsy because the earthly founder of their faith (Moses) and the heavenly founder of their faith (God) were absent. The people wanted something to hold (Remember the last chapter where I wanted something to hold that reminded me of my mother).

> **When the people saw that Moses was so long in coming down from the mountain, they gathered around Aaron and said, "Come, make us gods who will go before us ... Aaron answered them, "Take off the gold earrings that your wives, your sons and your daughters are wearing, and bring them to me." ... [Aaron took what they handed him and made it into an idol cast in the shape of a calf, fashioning it with a tool. Then they said, "These are your gods". Exodus 32:1-4**

The people wanted to have something to believe in, so they went to what they knew: worshiping animals like what the Egyptians did.

The hardest part of our faith is that we don't have a Moses, a Pillar of Fire at the Red Sea, or a Jesus. We have two things: a faith and a past of being in the world. Hebrews 11:1 tells us that "faith is confidence in what we don't see". Still, we are like the Israelites in that we want to hold onto something when we are lonely, scared, and bored, so we go back to what we knew from our previous life: animal worship. We go back to our first love, lying, stealing, jealousy, and every other form of sin. This is worshiping something other than God. To the Israelites, this straying led them to a cow; to us today, we are led to worship the world.

The Parable of the Sower talks about birds coming to steal the seeds that have fallen onto the path (Matthew 13:4). Jesus chose birds for a very specific reason. He could have used chipmunks or ants or any animal that is a herbivore, but he picked an animal that is often associated with the devil. Jesus explicitly states that the birds represent the "evil one" in Matthew 13:19. Revelations 18:2 is also an interesting parallel to birds and evil:

> **And he shouted with a mighty voice, saying, "Fallen, fallen [certainly to be destroyed] is Babylon the great! She has become a dwelling place for demons, a dungeon haunted by every unclean spirit, and an abode for every unclean and loathsome bird.**

Note that the verse mentions three things that will inhabit Babylon-the home of the antichrist and all evil found during and leading up to the Tribulation: demons, unclean spirits, and unclean birds. Demons are pretty straightforward, but let's dive into the unclean for a second. Unclean was used in the Bible as the result of actions that would preclude a Jew from worship activities or from entering the Temple. Unclean persons were not allowed to take part in celebrations. The Gentiles were considered unclean, so a good Jew was not allowed to go into a house or to eat with them. The Woman at the Well was shocked that Jesus would even talk to her since she was an unclean Gentile; Jesus was castigated by the religious leaders for interacting with the unclean tax collectors and sinners; Peter refused to eat unclean animals in his vision in Acts; and Paul went on a crusade to kill Christians because of their heretical (i.e. unclean) theology on Jesus.

Again, please don't check out by thinking that this does not apply to you because Revelations 18:4 might just show us how it does. Verse two just shows us how Babylon was the center of everything against God and verse four states that Christians were willing living with the evil birds/demons:

> **I then heard another voice from heaven saying, Come out from her, my people, so that you may not share in her sins, neither participate in her plagues.**

I checked over ten different translations, and each translation was identical in the phrase "come out". Usually, translations will have minute differences as Hebrew words can be translated into different English words (e.g. in Revelations 18:2 some versions stated home, some used abode, etc). I find the phrase "come out" to be very interesting as it indicates that the people were there of their own choice. The people were not prisoners in Babylon or exiled captives; if they had been, God would have used escape or some variant of escape. The believers and followers of God had willingly entered into Babylon to, as Revelations 18:3 states, indulge in the devil's luxuries and adulteries. God had watched His people leave to go back to the old life style.

I cannot stress enough that in the Last Days God's people will willingly choose to enter into the worship of the enemy- they will trade the worship of the one true God for the worship of "animals". This should not shock us, as the Church today is making the same choice. Honestly, wayward believers are not new: Israel had to be saved by numerous Judges because of straying, Israel and Judah were both exiled due to straying, the Temple was destroyed due to people straying, the Protestant Reformation was sparked because the leaders were straying, and the list could go for ever. Jesus came down to Earth because the people had, were, and would stray. It is a fact of life that "all have sinned and fallen short". All of us have fallen into the animal worship of the past.

The issue that I want to bring up now is an issue that I will expound upon more in the next chapter, where I discuss boundaries. My goal in this chapter is to hammer the fact that we willingly worship things that we should not because we start straying. Our straying blinds us to the truth and leads us to worship something that we should not worship. This worship can take many different forms, but the most dangerous are barely even noticed.

We can look back now and realize that the Catholic Church was wrong for excommunicating the scientist Galileo for stating that the Earth revolved around the sun. We can realize that Joan of Arc is a story of politics and not of religion. For those that do not know her story, Joan was burned at the stake for wearing men's clothes when she fought for the French. The French were all about this young girl hearing "from God" as her reason for fighting for the French. Of course, the English stated that she was hearing from "demons". The history of Medieval Europe is one where the Church was more of a political entity than a religious one. The interesting thing is that most people were semi unaware of the truth because everything religious was in Latin and few common people understood Latin. The people were ignorant of truth and blindly following the leaders of the day, who were indulging in quests for power and pleasures.

Revelations 18:3 states that the leaders of the world will indulge in the adulteries of Babylon (animal worship), and it is easy to see from the next verse that the people will blindly follow them again. This time the people cannot blame the lack of linguistic ability to understand the Bible. Instead, we have been swayed by science to discount the Bible. I cannot tell you how many Christians that I run into that believe in the Theory of Evolution. This is true heresy as Evolution directly contradicts God's creation. The Bible states that God created every animal in Genesis 1:25 where the phrase "all the creatures that move along the ground". It also states that God created man and woman. Yet, we want to believe that animals crawled out of the oceans and evolved into animals that would evolve into animals that would evolve into animals that would evolve into humans. We take Creation away from God and give it to animals. By believing in Evolution, we make animals our creator.

When you hear someone say that they were healed from a sickness, you have to decide whether to credit science or God. Now, I am not disclaiming the works of antibiotics. I have made use of them numerous times in my life and have given props to Alexander Fleming for discovering penicillin. Still, there are times when the doctors are flummoxed, when modern medicine fails, or when things just go away without logical explanation. I have watched believers and non-believers write this off to coincidence. We have stopped believing in miracles and want to find scientific answers to life.

I was having dinner with a couple of fellow believers one day, and the wife started recounting a story about how a person had wronged her daughter. She used a cuss word to describe the person. The husband gave his wife a look, to which she responded, "What, did I curse? Well, she is a [curse word]". The husband laughed it off in agreement. This is not an isolated situation in churches today. We trivialize Biblical passages as we stray further and further from the field and onto the path. The Bible becomes "well that was for the olden days" or "that word does not mean this; it actually means something else that allows me to do what I want". Each time, birds (the devil) come in and steal the messages, the warnings, and the truth that God is trying to impart on your life. In essence, you are denying the very truth that should be building up your Hedge and making a substitution of lies, empty promises, and rubbish.

Unfortunately, my rescuer had to put down his dog. It broke the family emotionally, but the dog attacked their child. No one will be happy with the outcome of that story- everyone was hurt. This is the point though- we get hurt when we put things into situations and roles that they were not meant to see. Animals were made to be watched and cared for by humans, not to be worshiped. My family gives me a lot of grief for sleeping on the couch to avoid disturbing the cat. Everyone else just moves the cat over and claims their bed or their pillow. The cat gives them an affronted stare and stalks off, but she forgives them in the morning. The cat understands that she is not the master and that humans are supposed to be in charge. I suppose that I should learn the same and not let the reproachful looks bother me.

Did you discount most of what I said when I discussed animal worship?

Do you see how going back to your old lifestyle choices is a form of "animal worship"?

What are areas of your life where you have slipped back into your old ways?

What do you need to do to have a better Hedge?

The Hedge as Caution Tape

Years ago, I lived at a Christian fraternity house. Our house was situated on a corner that marked the edge of the college and the start of fraternity/sorority row. Basically, anyone that belonged to Greek life or lived close to campus walked by our house. People cut through our driveway about a million times a day, which was cool that they had to at least see the sign that marked us as Christians, but it also brought us into conflict with one of our roommates.

John grew up in a small rural area where hunting was almost a religion unto itself, and he took bow hunting more seriously than he took his schoolwork. One day, John showed up with some caution tape and an idea. John commented that his second-floor bedroom window was the same height off the ground as the tree stand that he hunted from back home. He bought the caution tape to stretch across our driveway to block it off when he would practice firing arrows from his window at targets in our parking lot. Shockingly for a group of nine college guys that were barely 20 years old, we actually thought this might not be the best idea. We tried to tell John that this was probably illegal and, if not, still a bad idea. We guaranteed that someone would get an arrow through their cranium, landing him in jail for involuntary manslaughter.

John was adamant that the caution tape would keep people away from our yard and that it was safe to practice. No amount of logic would convince him that college students wouldn't care about caution tape, wouldn't notice caution tape, or would probably see it as a line in the sand that had to be crossed. It's human nature to want to go where we know that we shouldn't go. It is as old as Adam and Eve being cast out of the Garden of Eden. There is something in us that fights authority or restraints.

This is where the Hedge comes back into play. The Hedge of Protection as we view it is more about keeping external threats out of our yard, but this misses that a hedge has two faces: the outside and the inside. The Hedge protects one from oneself. I mentioned before the idea of convictions and the setting of boundaries to keep yourself as far away from sin as possible. Our society no longer talks about convictions, or it labels them as legalistic barriers that man has erected to add onto what God commanded, as if we knew better than God. There is some truth that the Holiness Movement did stray into legalism and turned some away from the faith. Yet the alternative that we now embrace is the Seeker Friendly Movement where sin, Hell, and punishment are not mentioned and where the Cross is no longer gracing the walls of the church. The Seeker Friendly Movement has very legitimate foundations: Jesus was seeker friendly, but this movement has also gone astray and has pushed people away from the truth.

At this moment, how would you describe your hedge? Is it thick or thin?

Do you lean more Seeker Friendly or Holiness Movement in your walk?

Too often, the church today has placed caution tape along their life thinking that this will keep them from falling away. Caution tape does tell us to stay away, but the same part of us that makes us question authority, speed on the freeway, and eat all of the chips when we know that we should save room for dinner makes it so caution tape is too weak of a hedge. In old times, hedges were made up of a variety of different shrubs, trees, and, most importantly, thorns. In order for us to actually listen, there usually must be a good reason- like it's going to hurt if we do not. Why don't I go 100 mph on the freeway? I don't want to lose my license and pay a huge fine. Why do I make my house payment? Because the bank will repo my house and put me out on the street. Deterrents work wonders to keep us in line. Thorns in the hedge do an amazing job of keeping us from straying where we should not go.

Our Hedge will keep us safe in several ways, if we build it up properly. First it helps keep us safe from the **Image of Impropriety**. This is a conviction to not look like the world and to look more like the One that came to save the world. Those of you that grew up listening to Christian music during the 90s are probably familiar with DC Talk. One of their greatest songs, *What if I Stumble*, starts with a quote theologian/author Brennan Manning:

> **The greatest single cause of atheism in the world today is Christians who acknowledge Jesus with their lips, then walk out the door and deny him by their lifestyle. That is what an unbelieving world simply finds unbelievable.**

While you may have heard of DC Talk, I am guessing that you have never heard of the Christian punk band called The Blamed; they made a song, called *No Difference*, about the same time. The chorus of the song made a big impact on my life and shaped how I eventually decided to build my Hedge.

> **What should I do?**
> **No difference between me and you.**
> **Why be a Christian**
> **If I'm just like you**

Both lyrics talk about the overwhelming need for us Christians to be a City on a Hill, the Salt of the Earth, a Lamp on a Stand. Our lives are called to be living testimonies that bring the truth to the world. In 2 Corinthians 8:21, we are told to live the Light, holy action, not just before God but before man as well. There can be no double mindedness or difference between how we are in different settings. We are supposed to show our faith everywhere we go.

The Bible is very clear that we are supposed to live a life that is blameless. The Apostle Paul instructs Titus (2:6-8) to encourage the young men to be self-controlled, to set an example of doing what is right, and to live in such a way that no one could find a fault in what they did or how they lived. The more we look like the world, the less we look like God. There are no two ways about it. God said that in the end, He will separate the sheep and the goats and that only one set goes to Heaven; remember, many on that day will cry out to the Lord saying that they followed Jesus only to be told that they are goats and were never known as children of God.

Be honest, how would a non-believer grade your behavior (A you shine the light of God to all to E where you look exactly like a non-believer)

What is one area of your life where you look a lot like God's representative?

What is one area where you look more like the world?

What steps do you need to improve your grade?

The second way that a Hedge protects us is that it prevents us from lingering in **Bad Behavior**. In 3 John 1:11, we are told that we are not to imitate evil, and 1 Thessalonians 5:12 tells us to abstain from evil. In both cases, the use of the term of evil is very intentional. Life is kind of black (sin) and white (holiness). There aren't really gray issues; you either imitate God or evil. I think that there is a reason that the third chapter of James goes into so much depth about the tongue. Our mouth gets us into so much trouble and shows people very clearly what is in our hearts. The words we say, the stories we tell, the interests that we share are a clear looking glass into the health of our heart, for the mouth spits out what is inside us.

One of the ways that we cheapen our Hedge is a misinterpretation of Scripture (Remember, scripture was misquoted to Jesus during his temptation in the wilderness). Jesus said that it isn't what goes into our body that makes us unclean but what comes out. Too many of us have taken this as free reign to get rid of convictions and barriers. This makes no sense because what we bring into ourselves shows where the heart is and leaves us vulnerable to straying. It would be like me saying to my wife, "Yes, I know that I frequent a prostitute every night, but I never tell her I love her. So, I'm not unfaithful right?". Everyone would be perfectly fine with my wife leaving me because my heart is being shown by my actions. Our mouth shows our heart, and our mouth shows what appetites that our heart desires. When our heart desires God, we consume things that are good, holy, and right, but our heart leads us to consume things that are ungodly when we stray outside the boundaries that our Hedge is supposed to keep us from heading.

What is your heart yearning to consume?

What would God say if He sat down to watch TV with you, to read the book you chose, to listen to your conversation, etc? Would he be shocked or pleased?

Convictions are not popular, but they are crucial. They help us by providing the third function of the Hedge: **Being In the World but not Of the World**. The Hedge is not supposed to keep us out of the world. Our great commission is to be a light to the world, and the only way to be a light is to be seen. We cannot hide, but we also cannot live as the world does. There might be no harder thing in our Chrisitan walk than finding that balance; the world wants to creep into our life and entice us away from a godly path. One of the most troublesome passages of Scripture for the Holiness Movement is probably when Jesus was at the Wedding at Galilee in John 2. I am not going to get into the legality of drinking, the benefits of not drinking or drinking, or anything on this topic. I do want to point out something very interesting, though. When the wine ran out, Mary had to go find Jesus to tell him of the problem. While from a spiritual sense Jesus knew that this was going to happen, it is important to note that He wasn't next to the festivities and the wildness going on at a wedding- He was at the celebration without being a "part of it".

This dual nature of Christian walk is very hard. Every time that Jesus was faced by worldly forces, He went behind his Hedge. Think of the Feeding of 5000; after Jesus fed everyone, the crowd wanted to make Him a worldly king. This was not His calling, so He left and went into the mountains to pray. How many times do you see Jesus do miracles, teachings, and works to only go into a quiet place to reconnect with God and get himself squared away to be in the world without being a part of it? Just before His arrest, Jesus went to God and prepared Himself for the path that He was about to take. I don't think that Jesus was really looking forward to a Roman flogging, carrying a cross through the streets while being scorned, or the painful death awaiting. When He was tempted to walk outside of God's path, Jesus went into His safe place and got himself squared away. Our Hedge is where we have to go to protect ourselves from falling too far into the world.

How often do you hunker down behind your Hedge and seek to make sure that you're in a right walk with God?

<u>Really look at your life and decide what percentage of you is in the world and what percentage is a part of the world.</u>

Finally, the **Hedge keeps us from Judging**. When Peter had his vision about eating unclean animals, Peter's struggle wasn't in listening to God. Remember the lesson that God was trying to get him to understand about going to the Gentiles and bringing the Light to them, but Peter was struggling with the appearance of defiling himself. Jews at this time did not even want to talk to a Gentile and so become unclean. This is an extension of being in but not part of the world. We must be careful not to call people unclean. Actions are unclean; people are God's children: prodigal and redeemed alike. In the Sermon on the Mount, Jesus warned about murder, but He completely turned the idea of murder upside down when he claimed that anyone that hated his brother was guilty of being a murder. Some have tried to soften this by saying that "brother" refers to a Christian. This is legalism and a desire to justify our sins. Each person is formed in God's image by God himself. Every human is a "brother" in one sense, so we are called to love everyone. Jesus didn't come to call the righteous, but He came to give His life for the forgiveness of sins, which as Paul pointed out is every one of us.

It shocks me how often I have heard Christians say that they hate someone because of their lifestyle. Hating gay people, drug users, adulterers, etc is no more or less godly than practicing witchcraft or stealing or using the Lord's name in vain. All sin is sin. The Bible says that the measure that we use will be used against us. Matthew 18 illustrates this perfectly with the Parable of the Unforgiving Servant. The servant who was forgiven much was unwilling to forgive a small debt. There is a reason that the Lord's Prayer has "forgive us our trespasses as we forgive those who trespass against us" and the Sermon on the Mount asks how we can take a speck out of someone's eye when we have a plank in our own.

I will be honest that the last part of the Hedge is the one where I struggle the most. I grew up in a family that was suspicious of others. My dad had the mindset where you should hate others because they were untrustworthy and deserved to be hated. My insecurities led me to my motto: hate them before they can hate you. The letters from John are clear: God is love. We are called to love like He loved. Jesus gave His life for the very person that I hated. It's my plank that I am working to remove.

<u>Are you like me and struggle with accepting this part of the Hedge or is there a different aspect?</u>

<u>Is there someone or some group that has drawn your hatred? What can you do to right this?</u>

I used to spend a lot of time in my grandpa's woods. He had a short 80 acres, and I roamed almost all of them. I would have pretend wars and fight battles at Fox Den Hill (an old fox den) and at the Cattail Patch. I would hold the line at the boundary of our woods against invaders and would patrol the marsh to make sure no one tried crossing it. In all, I knew every inch of every acre by heart except for one area. Oddly, this area was bordered by my favorite spot in the woods, but it was blocked to me by a patch of thorns. I tried to venture near it and got several burning scratches. That one experience was enough for me. The hedge kept me from wandering into this area. For illustrative purposes, I am going to say that this area was full of poison ivy, a bear den, and a dangerous drug cartel's home. Well, maybe not. Then again, I don't know because I never went there. The thorns did a great job of doing their job.

It is important to see that the thorns that keep evil on the outside are the same thorns that require us to be prepared when we leave the Hedge. In order for our faith to not be choked by the thorns mentioned in the Parable of the Sower, we must have protection from thorns (inside and outside of the Hedge). In another chapter, I will mention how the Shield of Faith is our portable Hedge. In order to leave our safe place with God, we must gird ourselves with faith. How do we blend the Holiness Movement and the Seeker Friendly Movement into something that God would view with pride: we have a mature faith that protects us from everything that could entangle our walk.

Overall, how solid and thick is your hedge? Is it ornamental/ sentimental like my stuffed animals Ribbie and Garfield or does it have some thorns?

How willing are you to heed your Hedge and not go where you don't belong?

In the end, we were able to talk John into abandoning his plan. No arrow flew from the house. I wish I could say that it was my unassailable logic and fiery oratory skills that swayed John, but I can't claim credit. We had to threaten to tell the campus minister about the idea. Evidently, the campus minister was the impediment that could protect John from himself.

What do you need to do to have a better Hedge?

The Hedge as a Thirst Quencher

While many people remember the 1930s because of the high unemployment of the Great Depression, few people remember that this time period also saw the greatest ecological disaster of the 20th Century, perhaps ever. The Dust Bowl was so named for the swirling dust storms that hit the Great Plains, specifically Oklahoma. Topsoil eroded and was swept up by prairie winds; the winds created dust storms so violent and so widespread that it blocked out the sun and caused lung problems. Cars were buried or shorted out by the intense static electricity that was built up, shocks so strong that they could knock a grown man off his feet. This was not solely restricted to the Great Plains though; Nebraska topsoil was found raining down on an ocean liner over 100 miles off the coast of New York harbor. The History Channel has a nice article on a 1934 storm that saw a two-mile-high dust storm travel over 2000 miles. It is estimated that one year later over 3000 tons of topsoil was lifted off the Great Plains in a single day, known as Black Sunday. The National Weather Service recorded that the dust was so thick that it was impossible to see one's own hand despite it being held within inches of the face.

The Dust Bowl's must be remembered for its major causes: poor farming practices. The focus on high priced crops, which often deplete soil nutrients, and poor farming technique led to soil that was easily exposed; perhaps this would have been less than damaging except for a decade-long drought that hit the country. The poor care of the land and the drought allowed prairie winds to run unchecked over the exposed soil and created the catastrophe recorded in John Steinbeck's Grapes of Wrath.

While farmers still struggle with weather, soil erosion, proper rainfall, and many other problems, techniques have been instituted to protect farmland from experiencing another Dust Bowl. Trees were planted to block wind. The hedge that was formed protected the soil from erosion but also from water evaporation. Land that lacks good water will dry up and become susceptible to dying, which leads to the ground losing the all-important topsoil. Topsoil is vital for crop growth; in fact, The Guardian ran an article stating that 95% of the crops grown in the world comes from topsoil.[3] The gardening site The Spruce goes further in stating the topsoil is "where the magic occurs".[4] Topsoil literally controls the fruitfulness of land and the ability for each person to survive.

Going back to the Parable of Sower, we see how evaporation has a spiritual application. We have already looked at how easy it is to get off the path and to be at the mercy of poor growing conditions and attacks from animals, but Jesus went on to express another issue with growing ability: topsoil and water.

> **Some fell on rocky places, where it did not have much soil. It sprang up quickly, because the soil was shallow. But when the sun came up, the plants were scorched, and they withered because they had no root ... The seed falling on rocky ground refers to someone who hears the word**

---

[3]   Cosier, Susan. (May, 2019). *The World needs Topsoil to Grow 95% of its Food.* The Guardian. https://www.theguardian.com/us-news/2019/may/30/topsoil-farming-agriculture-food-toxic-americ

[4]   Miller, Kathleen. (April, 2023). *Topsoil: What is it and How to use it in the Garden.* The Spruce. https://www.thespruce.com/what-is-topsoil

> **and at once receives it with joy. But since they
> have no root, they last only a short time. When
> trouble or persecution comes because of the
> word, they quickly fall away. Matthew 13:5-6
> and 20-21.**

At the most basic level, Jesus is talking about a spiritual dust bowl
in our hearts. We have no depth to our faith, so there is not enough
water and sustenance to keep us from being choked down by the
problems that we face. The key to avoiding choking is to create
healthy soil, which requires water.

The Bible talks about water in several places. The book of Revelations
shows imagery on the importance of water in our life, or what Jesus
speaks of in John 4 as Living Water. It is important to remember
that Revelations relies heavily on imagery to convey messages
about salvation and Heaven, so its words are vital to our faith. In
Revelations 21:6-8, God gives his famous quote about being the
Alpha and the Omega.

> **He said to me: "It is done. I am the Alpha and
> the Omega, the Beginning and the End. To the
> thirsty I will give water without cost from the
> spring of the water of life. Those who overcome
> will inherit all this, and I will be their God and
> they will be my children. But the cowardly, the
> unbelieving, the vile, the murderers, the sexually
> immoral, those who practice magic arts, the
> idolaters and all liars—they will be consigned
> to the fiery lake of burning sulfur. This is the
> second death.**

While we have all heard this said a million times, we often miss
the next part of the passage: the giving of living water. Living

water is given without cost to everyone who overcomes trials and tribulations and refuses to leave the faith. The word overcomes can also be translated persevere. The Bible is pretty straightforward about perseverance:

> **We rejoice in our suffering, knowing that suffering produces endurance and endurance produces character, and character produces hope, and hope does not put us to shame because God's love has been poured into our hearts. Romans 5:3-5**

The book of James, 1:2-4, goes on to tell us that we are to consider it pure joy when we face trials because it develops perseverance which makes us complete. While the Hedge does not give us water, the Hedge protects us from losing our water. The loss of perseverance precludes us from receiving living water and leads to drying up and withering away.

Plants cannot grow without water. People cannot live more than three days without water. There is nothing more important in the world than protecting our water source. Actually, there is nothing more important in the supernatural sense than protecting our water. Revelations 21 goes on to say that living water is not given to the cowardly, the idolaters, or the immoral. The punishment given to the people that are denied living water is a different water: the Lake of Fire, i.e. judgment.

We are told that living water comes from the very throne of God and that this river flows through Heaven and that fruit bearing trees spring up along its sides, whose leaves bring healing (Rev 22:1-2). Probably the coolest thing about this living water, aside from its sin cleansing power described in Rev 7:13-17, is that everyone that believes in Jesus can have this spring flowing from their hearts (John

7:38). Imagine yourself as having the very river that flows from God's throne flowing from your heart, watering everything that you touch in a way that it bears life giving fruit (the Fruits of the Spirit) and gives healing to those who come by you. Remember the woman that touched Jesus's garment and was healed from years of bleeding? Yeah, that healing power can come out of you as well.

Jeremiah 2:13 informs us that God calls himself the living water and this water in our lives is the very essence of God in us. Yet how many of us, me included, literally cause others to bear spiritual fruit and bring spiritual healing just by being near to us. Unfortunately, there are very few of us that have that much water flowing from us. We have a water problem. We have not protected our water: whether it be from allowing the world to evaporate by a lack of godliness or we have allowed our water source to be tainted. I'm not sure if you have ever played the old computer game The Oregon Trail. I am a huge history buff and love the game. It is fun to see if you can keep your family alive, but it is also fun to get the bad news of the Trail. I cannot tell you how many times Little Susie and Little Johnny died from dysentery. In a lot of cases, the game says, "You drank bad water and got dysentery".

The imagery from the Oregon Trail game is the same imagery of the Lukewarm Christian: being half in the world and half in Heaven causes a violent expulsion of the offender. For those of you that know what dysentery is will get how this imagery fits; those that do not should use a dictionary for a vivid mental picture of how this works. The quality of our water cannot be stressed enough. We either get eternal living water of healing and God or we get the burning water of judgment. It is that simple.

How do you keep from being overwhelmed by the world, especially early in your walk? "Easily", you must create a spiritual Hedge that protects your faith from being shallow. You must protect your water source. Your water source must first be abundant. Remember, the Dust Bowl happened in an unprecedented drought. Theologian Clarence Haynes Jr described the flow of the living water in John 7:38 as a flowing, moving powerful torrent of water and not the tiny trickle or stream that most of us have allowed to flow in our life. Growth comes from this powerful river. Every great early civilization started around a major river. The early Chinese civilization started between the Yellow and Yangtze Rivers, while India was centered around the Ganges River. The great early Egyptian Empire followed the Nile River. The Garden of Eden is thought to have been located in Mesopotamia (home to some of the great civilizations like Babylon and Assyria) between the Tigris and Euphrates Rivers. Great civilizations and advancement came from legitimate rivers, not pitiful streams. These are not shallow rivers. The Nile and Yangtze rivers reach depths of 30 feet, while the Ganges and Euphrates can reach depths of over 100 feet.

How strong is your water source?

If our ability to thrive and grow is related to the breadth of our river, then how happy are you with the depth of your river/stream/puddle?

I think that we have all been to a house or a hotel that lacks good water pressure. Showers in these locations are useless. Why? It is very hard to get clean when there is not enough water to cleanse your body of impurities. The living water flowing from us is the same way. How can we fulfill our Great Commission if our water pressure of our faith is low? A sickly flow is just that: sickly. In order for healing and growth, there has to be an abundance of water.

The quality of our water must also be protected. The prophet Jeremiah warned Israel that they were running after idols and would suffer the consequences for their disobedience. While he, and other prophets, used a ton of different images to show this idolatry, one of the more interesting cases is found in 2:18 where he condemns Israel for going to drink from the Niles and Euphrates rivers. In 2 Kings 5, Namaan went to Elisha for healing from leprosy and was told to bathe in the Jordan River. Namaan was affronted as the rivers back in his home were "better", but he missed the most important point about the water: healing/living water only comes from God. Not all water is built equally. Some will give you spiritual dysentery. Some will bring you to spiritual ruin. Some will produce a crop a hundred-fold and will bring complete healing.

As a society, we run after our healing from a lot of places. While there is nothing wrong with going to a doctor, the wrong comes from us placing all of our faith in science and no longer looking to God. We have become more enamored by the power of man and less by the Power of God. When was the last time that you heard of a miraculous healing? Did you even believe it or were you skeptical? As a society, we rarely hear of miracles anymore. Has our God changed or lost power? Not at all. The only explanation is that we changed as a people and that we no longer acknowledge His healing touch. We have denied the very effects of the River of Life flowing from God's throne. Man can only do so much, and there are times when science falls short. God can, and has, cure diseases that claim so many people in this scientifically advanced era.

<u>Where are you going for healing?</u>

<u>Where does your water source come from?</u>

<u>Do you even believe in miracles anymore?</u>

Understanding the miraculous power of water in our lives is paramount. It bears noting some things about water. Do you realize that water was created on the first day? Water was the building block of life and creation. The human body is 60% water and mentioned

722 times in the Bible, more than prayer is mentioned. When God decided to bring judgment on the world, he wiped out mankind with a flood of water. God could have used anything, but I wonder if He chose a flood because He wanted to call out the people of the Earth for their pitiful faith. Was this God saying, "This is the type of power that faith has at its fingertips"? In the Exodus, Israel walked through the very waters that would wipe out Pharaoh's army. We could talk off the baptism by water, but to me, the most telling importance of water was seen on the cross. When Jesus had died, they pierced his side to make sure that he was dead (oh foolish people that say Jesus had just "fainted") and blood and WATER flowed. We talk about the blood of Jesus washing away our sins, but we forget that the blood that flowed down Him was mixed with water.

In the end, to protect our ability to grow, we must keep our soil and our water from evaporating. The Hedge was the perfect way to keep these two things from being blown away by the problems of the world. The Dust Bowl destroyed lives because of the lack of water for years of drought. Our faith will be destroyed without the living water.

The Hedge of Humanity

Somewhere around 30 years ago, a guest pastor came and spoke at my church. I wish I could remember his name or the names of his friends, but these particulars are inconsequential to the story. The consequential details to you and to me were those in the story he told about prayer. One morning, he felt the strong need to pray for a missionary friend that was stationed in Africa. So urgent was the need that the pastor got on the phone and called nine of his friends to immediately start praying for the missionary.

The need was, in fact, urgent. The missionary was on his way, through the jungle, back to the small village where he lived. He had walked all day to a bigger city to get costly medical supplies for the village. Unbeknownst to the missionary, a small group of individuals followed the missionary into the jungle with the plan to wait for the missionary to go to sleep in order to rob him. Some of the city toughs even suggested killing the missionary to keep it quiet. The urgent need to pray for the missionary came to the pastor as the missionary was setting up camp and falling asleep.

This story contains three people- the missionary, the pastor, and the pastor's posse, and each person is a metaphor for us- being alone, being in solitude, and constructing a hedge. The Bible gives us figures that can give deeper clarity how this plays out in our life.

The Bible has interesting things to say about solitude and about being alone. Solitude is supposed to be for prayer and for revelation; being alone is often an invitation to be attacked by an enemy. Recent events in society show just how devastating being alone can be to people. The year 2020 psychological trauma in our society. Regardless of the benefit that lockdowns may or may not have had, people are not meant to be isolated. We are social creatures and require some amount of interaction. The impact of being isolated from society led to too much time being spent on social media discussions, where nothing positive was conveyed. The amount of vitriol spewed on forums and chats illustrated that people will devolve into behaviors that they would not demonstrate in public, but society became angrier and more likely to slander, to backstab, and to hurt others. The danger for the missionary was that he was alone and, therefore, that he lacked protection and was open to the attacks of others.

Nehemiah is probably a figure that not a lot of us read about in the Bible. He is an Old Testament figure that lived during the time of the forced exiles and the Fall of the Temple. By all accounts, Nehemiah was doing well as the king's cupbearer. The cupbearer was one of the most important people in keeping the king safe. Nehemiah would closely monitor every drink that was served in parties to the king. He would also be asked to sample the wine to prove its safety. Moreover, the cupbearer would be at the king's side during discussions, therefore in the know of what was going on in the kingdom. The king would have to have absolute trust in the cupbearer for his very life- and Nehemiah was this man. Here Nehemiah was on top of the world, yet he felt alone. Have you ever been alone in a crowd? One of the biggest complaints about churches today is that people do not feel connected. People feel alone at work, at school, and in daily life. Nehemiah was immersed in a crowd of courtiers, sycophants, and officials all day long; still, he was so alone that the king noticed that something was amiss.

Look at what happened to the prophet Elijah after his big victory at Mt. Carmel. Remember, Elijah single handedly took on 400 prophets of Baal. This was a huge victory for God, and Elijah was a hero. It is interesting that the Bible states that when the fire came from Heaven and burned up the sacrifice on God's altar, as well as the water in the trough around the altar, that the people started chanting, "The Lord- he is God! The Lord- he is God!" I came across this passage a couple of days ago and was struck by this phrase. Elijah's name means "the Lord is God". While not the same, it is easy to see where the crowd was almost chanting something that sounded like "Elijah! Elijah!" This was a huge moment for Elijah in victory and as he got to tell the king that God would end a severe famine. Elijah should have been on cloud nine, yet Elijah goes off on his own Mt. Horeb and suffers an emotional breakdown. He actually begs for death. This man that was part of miracles greater than any since Moses, this man who was considered in Jewish history to be on a tier with Moses, this man who was believed to come back to usher in the Messiah was alone and so worn out that he was done living.

A close look at the prophet Jonah also shows what trouble comes to us when we are alone. Jonah was given an enviable task: go to the wicked city of Nineveh and get them to turn away from their wickedness. This was not just a go over and tell your family member to get right- the Ninevites were not Jews. This is huge for a variety of reasons. First, the city was the center of the Assyrian Empire. The Assyrians had their own gods, not Israel's God. The Assyrians would attack Israel and Judah in an effort to destroy or control them. I love the Veggie Tales version of Jonah as the Ninevites are referred to as people who would slap each other with fish. While fish slapping is probably not something that happened, the Ninevites were not a group of people that a good Jew would associate with for a million reasons. Yet, God called Jonah to go to Nineveh, and as we know, Jonah took off the other way- he went off on his own. Jonah knew that he was in the wrong and put a group of sailors at risk by sailing with them. When a big storm came and threatened to sink the ship, Jonah was by himself as the sailors were trying to save their lives. It wasn't until all the crew and passengers came together that Jonah came clean. The story continues to show that Jonah would go to the people of Nineveh who listened to him, but Jonah would go off on his own and complain that God was forgiving the Ninevites. Alone- Jonah wanders. With people- Jonah does the right thing.

Think back to the story of Bathsheba. Instead of being off to war with his troops, David stayed behind in Jerusalem and went off on his own, where he would see Bathsheba- who was alone and away from her husband, embark on an affair, lose a child, and have a man killed. He made decisions that would lead to an epidemic killing almost 100,000 people. He made a decision that would lead to a revolt by his own son. Alone, David was a wreck.

No greater illustration of the dangers of being alone can be shown than the Temptation of Christ. We know that Jesus was in the desert for 40 days and then was jumped by the devil. Jesus had finished praying and fasting and was ready to go back into the world. At that moment, Jesus was as vulnerable and as alone as He ever would be, and he was attacked at that moment. Jesus was tempted with twisted Bible verses and twisted promises of God. Of course, we know that Jesus did not succumb to these temptations, but what we forget to realize is that the devil knew that this was the one time that Jesus was truly "alone".

Being alone does this to us. We lose our support and our way when we go alone. Jesus showed us that our alone time is not meant to be alone- it is solely meant to recharge us and to prepare us for trials. He went off on his own after miracles, after teachings, and after times when people wanted to make Him king. I always wonder if Jesus went off by himself to be with God in order to remind Himself of the plan and to avoid getting in the way of this plan. The devil tried to get Jesus to go beyond Himself and take up God's role. Doesn't the enemy do that to us as well? How often do we pursue our plans and how often do we really consult Him? How often do we take credit for our successes and how often do we give God the glory for giving us the ability to succeed? Pride is always a step away from entering into our mind and making us try to make ourselves more than what we are. Did Jesus go off by Himself to help restructure His thoughts to make sure that He didn't get wrapped up in the world's will? Maybe not. Maybe. What we know for sure is that Jesus went off by Himself to get centered with God, whatever that meant for Jesus.

Before Elijah would have his greatest moment, at Mt. Carmel, Elijah spent three years in solitude preparing for what was to come. During this time, Elijah was fully relying on the Lord- ravens were literally flying in his meal every day. Think back to Elijah on Mt. Horeb where he met God. God knew that Elijah was weary, so He met with Elijah one on one before sending him off. God basically said, "You saw me and have been given what you need. Now get back in the game son. You are going to do great things." Yes, Elijah did great things with that pep talk: he did after all anoint a couple of kings. Still, the greatest help to Elijah though came in the form of a successor, a helper, a friend: Elisha. God used Elijah's time in solitude to build him up to be ready to go back into public, with the support of Elisha.

Nehemiah knew that being with God's people was what he needed to revive his spirit. The king noticed Nehemiah's melancholy and sent Nehemiah back to Jerusalem, where the Temple had been rebuilt. Nehemiah wanted to be back with believers and with the chance to worship at the Temple. Changing alone to solitude with God was hardly unique to Jesus, Nehemiah, and Elijah. Moses went up to meet God alone numerous times. During these times, Moses would be instructed by God on how to lead His people and how to live a godly life. Daniel was thrown into the lion's den because he went off in solitude to pray to God. Solitude is never alone. Solitude is prayer time, and prayer time is your time with God-together.

Still, being alone and in solitude is meant for a season or a time, but we are not called to be recluses. Think about Creation. God created the world and then Adam, but God was not happy that man would be alone. God knew that people need people. People get stronger as they increase in number.

> **Two are better than one,**
> **because they have a good return for their labor:**
> **If either of them falls down,**
> **one can help the other up.**
> **But pity anyone who falls**
> **and has no one to help them up.**
> **Also, if two lie down together, they will keep warm.**
> **But how can one keep warm alone?**
> **Though one may be overpowered,**
> **two can defend themselves.**
> **A cord of three strands is not quickly broken.**
> **Ecclesiastes 4:9-12**

God knew that Adam would be better with Eve, and vice versa. Community was very important to the early church. The disciples met daily to share food, to pray, and to encourage. The Bible states that God is where two or more are gathered (Matthew 18:20). It would seem that people are part of our Hedge.

Nehemiah is not remembered for leaving comfort and security; he was remembered for leaving that situation to go back and rebuild the wall around Jerusalem. This was important because the people were afraid of the surrounding people, which was impacting their worship. Nehemiah did not rebuild the wall alone though; he had each family repair a portion of the wall. In essence, each person put their blood, sweat, and toils into the wall, becoming the wall. The Hedge was a Hedge of People as much as it was a wall of stone.

Neil Diamond wrote a song that many saw as heretical but was meant to convey a deeply religious experience that he witnessed. The song, Brother Love's Traveling Salvation Show, has lines that have always spoken to me:

> **I said brothers**
> **Now you got yourself two good hands**
> **And when your brother is troubled**
> **You gotta reach out your one hand for him**
> **'Cause that's what it's there for**
> **And when your heart is troubled**
> **You gotta reach out your other hand**
> **Reach it out to the man up there**
> **'Cause that's what he's there for**

It is an interesting add on to the Nehemiah story. He used one hand to hold tightly to God, but then he used the other to grab ahold of the people near him.

Jesus knew this well and created the Twelve Disciples as a special group to be with Him. We know that Jesus had many people following Him. Why did He have an inner circle? Because Jesus understood that our friends, family, and acquaintances form a hedge around us. They protect us from our pride, our carelessness, and our ignorance. They protect us from not seeing the truth of our actions. Jesus also knew that one layer of people is not enough.

Just having layers of people in our life is not enough. We can still be vulnerable behind our Hedge of People and can be seen in the parallel of two princes and how they addressed situations.

Rehoboam, son of Solomon, became king of a unified Israel upon his father's death. Rehoboam did a wise thing when the people came to him and asked for the new king to relax the forced labor of Solomon. Let's unpack this request for a minute. Solomon was considered the wisest person in the world, and he was the builder of the Temple of the Lord. The labor used to build the Temple was not the problem, nor was it probably the building of Solomon's palace. Solomon was a massive builder, and we know that he had a palace built for Pharaoh's daughter. Who knows how many palaces he had built for his 1000 wives/concubines; what is known is that it was taxing on the people to build things that would become less about what God ordained and more about self-aggrandizement. Rehoboam had to make a choice: give into the people with his first decision or show his almighty power. Rehoboam started out on the right path. He went to the experienced advisors of Solomon, and he went to young people. Rehoboam started out with what looked like a solid group of advisors, but his advisors gave differing advice. This was actually a blessing in disguise. When we have a disparate group of people forming our Hedge, we are required to use the Hedge for its intended purpose.

The second prince was Jesus. He was also given a hard choice: suffer death on the cross or use His power to escape a graphic death. Jesus had his Twelve Disciples go with Him to the Garden of Gethsemane, but He did a peculiar thing: he took Peter and the sons of Zebedee off alone. If you remember the story, Jesus took the three off to the side and left them to go pray. He came back and chided the three for "not keeping the watch". Jesus had his protection, and He had it multi-layered: the disciples, the three, and then one on one with God. Jesus had a Hedge of people around Him to keep watch with Him. Keep watch over what though? Did Jesus need physical protection? Of course not. He chided Peter for chopping the ear off of a servant during the arrest as He could have called legions of angels to His defense. Jesus wanted His inner circles to keep the spiritual watch with Him. Jesus knew that being alone leads to temptation, and He did not want that extra temptation before the Cross. Jesus wanted a physical barrier against temptation but went into solitude to be with the Lord.

Rehoboam missed that final crucial piece of the Hedge. He had multiple layers of advisors, but he never sought the solitude to be in God's will and he did not make sure that his innermost circle was godly. Rehoboam would make a grievous error and would answer the people harshly and crudely. The Kingdom of Israel would be torn apart and lead to years of war. Jesus went a better path by adding prayer into His Hedge, which brings us back to the story of the missionary in the jungle.

We left the missionary alone, asleep and about to be attacked by a group of thugs. The missionary slept through the night undisturbed and made it to his village with all of the medical supplies. A month later, the missionary went back to the city to get more supplies. One of the thugs ran up to him in the market and asked, "How did you get so many guards into the jungle without us seeing them?" The missionary was confused. The thug confessed the whole plan to the missionary but added something truly miraculous. The thug maintained that the missionary had ten guards stationed around him that were fully armed and terrifying to behold. Remember, there were ten men who were praying at the time that the missionary was about to be attacked. People are part of our Hedge, but praying people make our Hedge terrifying to our enemy. Jesus set up a double layered Hedge of disciples to help Him battle fear and anxiety. Jesus made a decision to follow the Father's will and go to crucifixion. This took extreme courage to do the right thing. Jesus, though, did not rely just on his multi-layered Hedge- He was behind it using solitude to pray earnestly. Do we have to fear temptation? Sure, we need to avoid arrogance and pride, but the fear should be small compared to the security we feel of a Hedge of people praying to keep us safe as we are on our knees praying.

Is there anyone that you need to remove from your Hedge of People to avoid a Rehoboam type mistake?

Is there anyone that you need to add to your Hedge to better protect your faith?

What do you need to do to have a better Hedge?

PART II

Inside the Hedge

Hedge of La La La

I remember telling people that I was going to quit most of my extracurricular activities. Most people were a little shocked and asked why I was choosing to walk away. I explained that I wanted to play college baseball and that I wanted to devote my time to pursuing that dream. Most people would give me an incredulous look and would blurt out, "You really think you can play college ball?". When I gave an affirmative, I would receive a condescending smile.

In fairness, they had valid reasons to doubt my dreams. My freshman saw very little playing time and zero accolades for what I did accomplish. My sophomore year was a good year despite the fact that I was only the number one pitcher because the players ahead of me were injured or had quit; plus, I was passed up during the postseason run for players that were below me on the depth chart. My junior year saw me relegated to the deep bench. I was going into my senior year, and this was my last chance to make a name for myself. Honestly even if I had a decent year, there was very little likelihood of me being noticed because we had several kids that were stars and would garner all the attention. I was faced with a decision: I could listen to the naysayers and focus on how daunting the task was, or I could put on my noise canceling headphones and go for it.

Just like I had a naysayer doubting my ability, David faced a similar situation regarding Goliath. Everyone thought that the task was too difficult for David. He was the youngest of his brothers, and therefore the least. You might think that I am being harsh to David, but remember when the prophet Samuel came to the home of Jesse to anoint a king? Jesse paraded all his sons before Samuel except one: David. Jesse was ready to have dinner with an honored guest, and David was not even allowed to attend. I am guessing that some might say something about how the sheep needed to be protected and could not be left alone. True but, David was sent by his father to visit his brothers at the front lines in 1 Samuel 17, and we are told that David was able to leave the sheep with a shepherd. Let this sink in for a second, David was not important enough to be allowed a substitute shepherd to meet an important religious figure but was used to run food to his brothers. This clearly shows how Jesse viewed David's importance.

Things at the battlefront took a similar path. He was scolded by his brothers for wanting to help Israel defeat a giant that was mocking God. Saul was less than impressed at first sight of David despite David's assurances that he could take Goliath.

> **Saul replied, "You are not able to go out against this Philistine and fight him; you are only a young man, and he has been a warrior from his youth." I Samuel 17:33**

At this point, David gives his resume: I've fought a bear and a lion. I admit, I'm impressed. David might just be the toughest guy anywhere, but King Saul still tries to dress David in armor. Why? Because Saul still looked at David and could not look beyond what David was: a young boy that was not the hero that Saul was hoping to get. Goliath looked at David and had a similar reaction- this is really the best the Israelites have to send against me. Goliath was affronted that he had to lower himself to fight a little pretty boy.

Esther might not have had the people speaking down about her to her face, but she also faced her own fears about being able to do the job.

Esther was faced with a difficult task: save an ethnic group that King Xerxes had just condemned to death. Let's unpack what obstacles she faced. First, Esther was a member of the race that was supposed to be put to death, so by legal standards, she was basically an outlaw for being alive. Second, there was a rule that a person could be put to death for entering the king's presence without permission.

At this point, I assume someone will point out that Esther was the queen. Sure, she was the queen, but the previous queen was kicked to the curb and banned from ever seeing Xerxes again. The first chapter of Esther tells us that Vashti was not killed, but this was hardly a kind gesture. Banishment meant that Vashti would live in the harem for the rest of her life and be unable to pursue another marriage, go to her family, or have a purpose for her life- she was condemned to a life of loneliness. Esther had to be familiar with Vashti's fate and be fully aware that she could suffer the same. Plus, it is not like the queen even was the only woman in Xerxes' life. Remember, Solomon had a thousand wives and concubines. Legend has it that Xerxes had a concubine for each day of the year. Esther had a legitimate worry that she was not important enough to impact her environment.

No one probably had more of a reason to doubt their situation than Job. Job lost everything. He lost his ability to make money. He lost his children. He lost his health. Unfortunately, Job lost his support group. During hard times, people usually come out of the woodwork to comfort and help the afflicted. Job's wife tells him to curse God and die in Job 2. Wow, and I thought that my wife and I had some bad moments.

> **Anyone who curses his God will bear the consequences of his own sin, because the one who blasphemes the name of the LORD is certainly to be put to death. The entire congregation is to stone him to death. Leviticus 24:14-15**

Let me translate Job's wife's statement for you. She is asking Job to purposefully do an act that will incite a crowd to seize him, drag him to an area, and pelt him with stones until internal bleeding and cranium damage ends his life. I get that Job and his wife just lost everything, but she is almost asserting that Job's only use to her was to provide her with a pampered life and that he did not deserve to live once that good life was taken from her.

Job's plight gets worse as his good friends show up. Instead of consoling, the three friends spend the next thirty plus chapters telling Job that he had it coming and to just admit that he is a horrible person. I want you to imagine that you just lost every physical object that you own, lose your children (if you don't have them then get rid of your parents/cousins/aunts and uncles), lose your health to a degree where you just scrape your body with sharp objects to find relief, and have the love of your life abandon you. Now, take your three best friends and imagine them telling you that you deserved all of this.

All three of these Biblical figures are similar in that people doubted them and that the peanut gallery was quite vocal in these doubts. They had a similar choice that I had to make: listen to the naysayers and give up or yell "La, La, La" as loud as possible and go for redemption. Obviously, we know that these three went La, La, La and became some of the biggest heroes of our faith. To do this, each of them had to find a way to ignore the distractions and the detractors. This is what our Hedge is for: noise canceling. One of the greatest modern-day uses of a physical garden hedge is that it blocks out noise and blocks out distracting people, traffic, etc from entering our domain. Our spiritual Hedge is meant to do the same for us.

Job is the guy that is known for having a "hedge" around him. We see how the devil slowly starts stripping away everything from Job. Most people wrongfully assume that the devil was stripping away

Job's Hedge, but this is not true. Our Hedge is not meant to be our physical comforts, our wealth, or our connections. Our Hedge is the spiritual bulwarks that we enact through praise, prayer, Bible reading, and faith. Job refused to go against his faith, refused to sin (see 2:10). Job was willing to accept the good and the bad in life. Job was able to withstand every single attack because he had a hedge that helped him endure the attacks. Job's Hedge was constructed from a life of righteous living, with a focus on blamelessness. As he was attacked by everyone that was meant to comfort him, Job stayed behind that Hedge and yelled a variant of La, La, La (well, he said that the allegations were lies, but I think that you can forgive this loose translation).

Job teaches us a valuable lesson about how to cancel the noise that comes from people: he relied on his relationship with God. Job was adamant that his relationship with God was not compromised by sin and wrongdoing. He was adamant that he had followed the laws and the expectations of a God-fearing man. He never relied on what he had built, but he focused on his love for God and the amount of faith that he had in God. When we are hit hard by the troubles of life, we focus on what we are losing or how the situation will impact our comfort. Job never worried about his comfort; he was content to scrape himself with potshards without blaming God. Job never worried about what he had lost:

> **Naked I came from my mother's womb, and naked I will depart.**
> **The LORD gave and the LORD has taken away; may the name of the LORD be praised. Job 1:21**

On top of focusing on our relationship with God, Job chose to ignore ungodly counsel. Sometimes, people lead us astray or encourage us to cast blame on others. Job would have none of it. He did not let the emotional situation distract him from his reliance on God. Job's faith was unshakable, as was God's love for Job. In duress, we have to follow Job's example by refusing to listen to anything that is contrary to what we know to be true about God. In Job's case, he refused to believe that he was being punished for sinning. Job's belief in his relationship with God was rock solid.

Esther shows us that we cannot discount who we are. God puts us where we need to be and equips us with the ability, ours or His, to accomplish whatever task he sets before us. God's will is going to get done no matter what, and our role is to do whatever part that we are called to do. You are placed wherever you work, you live, or you frequent for a reason. I don't know what it is, and you might not either. Esther was chosen to be queen and spent at least two years being prepped for her role as queen. Just like He had a plan for Esther, God has you here to do something to advance His kingdom. Esther was called to disregard the worries of being disciplined, ostracized, or humiliated in order to do something miraculous.

It is not wrong to be afraid of doing God's will. Sometimes, we are called to do things that are very uncomfortable, but we are still called to do it. You probably don't have to worry about being executed for following God's plan, but it wouldn't matter if you had to worry about it. Paul said it best in "to live is Christ; to die is gain". The worst outcome that Esther would have had was to go be with God, but the right action would make her one of the most renowned figures, let alone women, in the Judeo-Christian faith.

David teaches us that we never have to listen to what others say about us or about the task ahead of us. The warriors of Saul were not enough because they looked to their own power and to the power of the giant in front of them. Saul's warriors listened to Goliath extol his might and their lack thereof, and they listened to this day after day. God does not need us to be the coolest person, the smartest person, the biggest person, the toughest person, or anything else.

David rightfully remembered, and Saul's soldiers forgot, the story of Joshua seeing the giants in the Promised Land and responding with a "let's go- God's got this". God will provide the words, the might, and the charisma to accomplish the task. David was the right choice because he was affronted that anyone would mock his God. David was the right person because he refused to give in to fear. David was the right person because he was willing to be the person who refused to listen to why God won't do it, why God can't do it, or why we should run.

None of these paragons of faith were born with a special amount of faith. They had to build their faith. Esther was terrified to go before Xerxes. There is nothing wrong with being afraid of the task before you, but Esther's example was to go off and pray and fast. David had already spent his time tending the sheep and building his faith in God while being alone in the wilderness. Job prepared for his trial by constantly sacrificing and praying. In each case, you see that these heroes were off alone working on their relationship with God. They were behind their Hedge growing their faith. The Hedge allowed each of them to block on the noise and to focus on their relationship with God. Remember, a hedge's purpose is to allow things to grow.

Blocking out the noise of the naysayers, the experts, and the odds against us is one of the most vital roles of the Hedge. Often, God calls us to do things that just can't happen unless there is a miracle, and it is for this very reason why we have to get good at yelling La, La, La when confronted with a task that is impossible. We know that the task is impossible-for us. Thankfully, we aren't the ones actually accomplishing anything.

Think of how different the Bible would have been if people had listened to the naysayers or to the facts against them. Moses was afraid to go to Pharaoh. Anaias was rightfully hesitant to meet Saul. Ruth was told to go back to Moab. Rahab was probably hesitant to betray her people. The Bible would still have all these stories of the Plagues leading to the Exodus, someone becoming a Paul, and women who would become part of the genealogy of Jesus, but the difference is that the names would be different. As Mordecai told Esther in Esther 4:14, God's work will come regardless.

To have a faith strong enough to be ready to ignore the noise, we have to fully listen to God. There was not a stronger man in history than Samson, but there might not have been a man that was harder of spiritual hearing than Samson. Samson relied on Samson, which is what we default to as people; faith allows us to tune out every voice but God's.

Yelling La, La, La at the voices is rewarding beyond belief. I was able to tune out the voices that told me that I wouldn't achieve my goals in baseball. One of the greatest sports moments in my life was during my last game of my career when a college coach walked up to me and congratulated me and said the words "can't wait to coach you next year".

What areas of your life do you need to yell La, La, La to instead of listening?

How much do you really believe that God will provide you with everything that you need when the time comes?

Do you give into the lie that David, Esther, and Job were somehow super humans that had been given more strength, faith, or courage than you?

The Hedge on a Mountain

This may sound odd, but I am afraid of heights. Most people assume that tall people would love heights, but a lot of us don't. Maybe we live our life looking at how far down the ground is every day and know that a fall would hurt. I've seen trees fall, and they shake the earth when they hit. It doesn't look enjoyable. Then, you add going up on something taller still, and it just adds to the unease that us tall folk have.

Maybe this fear is why I did not want to go to Yellowstone National Park with its mountain passes, well that and the chance of being or having my children be eaten by a grizzly bear was not appealing. My dad always told me that he would take me to Yellowstone and drive on the Beartooth Highway. He would regale me with how he rode that highway as a youth and how he would hold his head out the window and look over the cliff hundreds of feet down. When I asked him if cars ever went over the edge, he would just laugh and say, "Yep, and that's where they stay".

My dad talked about us taking this trip for years; unfortunately, we never took this trip together. He passed away suddenly, and I was left with the knowledge that one of the reasons that we never took this trip is because of my fear. After he died, I decided to visit Yellowstone in his honor. I will admit that the fear of Beartooth Highway did not go away, but I wanted to experience the mountains that my dad talked about so much. I wanted to see the wildlife that my dad raved about seeing. I wanted to see Old Faithful and Grand Prismatic. I felt a call to go to the mountain to experience something life changing.

God also had a vision that he wanted the Israelites to experience. The Israelites had been taken away in exile and had lost their Temple where they worshiped God. They were taken to a land where the people acted, ate, lived, and worshiped differently. This was the land where the Israelites were almost wiped out but were saved by Esther. This was the land of Shadrach, Meshach, and Abendego being thrown in the fiery furnace. Life was not always easy. Life had moments where it took a lot of prayer and quiet time to endure. Still, God had a vision of something better- and it involved mountains. In Ezekiel 36:8, God states

> **But you, O mountains of Israel,**
> **you will put forth your branches and bear your**
> **fruit for My people Israel;**
> **for they will soon come**

This verse is rich in symbolism and meaning, so understanding it takes some unpacking. First, what is "the Mountains of Israel"? Second, how does a mountain bear fruit? For the moment, we are going to leave the latter question for a later chapter. In the early part of Ezekiel 36, and elsewhere in the Bible, Mountains of Israel can mean the Promised Land. The fourth verse of this chapter gives clarity when the Lord clarifies the Mountains of Israel as the hills, mountains, valleys, ravines, and towns that were destroyed when Jerusalem fell to the Babylonian armies.

God gave Ezekiel a message of encouragement that the exiled people would return to the Promised Land again and bear fruit; however, this is not why God chose to use Mountains of Israel instead of

Jerusalem, the Promised Land, or some other term. We have to assume that the decision to say that the Mountains of Israel was purposeful and meant to lead us to some deeper truth. In this case, the deeper truth lies in the role that mountains play in the culture of Israel and the culture of Israel's neighbors.

A recurring theme in the two Book of Kings is worship of gods at the high places. These high places were often mountain tops or a place that was higher than where a city/village was built. People would go to these high places and offer sacrifices to the local god in order to receive favor or forgiveness. The act of worship on these high places was condemned by God, who tasked the kings of Judah and Samaria with destroying these places of idolatry. The worship of the true God or false gods at the high places became a measuring stick for the moral compass of a king.

King Jeroboam is a noteworthy king because he is the person that divided the Israelites, into Judah and Israel, when he rebelled against Solomon's son Rehoboam. Rehoboam made a lot of bad decisions and came at a time when the Chosen People of God had just watched their king backslide into the worship of foreign gods, so it is not surprising that the majority of the country did not want anything to do with him. The ten tribes that broke away and chose Jeroboam to be their king, but fear and uncertainty still got the better of his decision making. Jeroboam was so afraid of his citizens going to Jerusalem and the Temple to worship God that he built high places in Bethel and Dan. Many people will remember that Jeroboam set up golden calves as idols to be worshiped as representatives of God, and many people will fixate on the "Sin of Jeroboam" as idol worship. This was obviously a huge part of his sin, but the idol was only part of his sin. The setting up of new high places that did not have the Ark of Covenant and sacred Holy of Holies was also a major sin.

King Asa of Judah was a solid king on the surface. The Bible tells us in 1 Kings 15 that

> **Asa did what was right in the eyes of the Lord, as his father David had done. He expelled the male shrine prostitutes from the land and got rid of all of the idols his ancestors had made ... Asa cut down [the Asherah pole] and burned it in the Kidron valley. <u>Although he did not remove the high places</u>, Asa's heart was fully committed to the Lord all his life. [Underlining is mine].**

Really, there is not much more that you could ask of Asa after following his father Abijah, who was described as a man who was not devoted to God and followed in the sins of his predecessors. Asa removed all signs of idol and false god worship, and he tried to get the hearts of Judah back on the right path. Still, Asa has the asterisk in his life: he did not remove the high places.

This asterisk was also given to some other great kings. Joash was one of the longest serving kings of Judah, 40 years in all. He rebuilt the Temple of the Lord so that the people could worship the Lord properly; unfortunately, 2 Kings 12 tells us that he allowed the high places to remain. It is important to note that these high places were in Judah, so the golden calves were not a part of this worship. The high places here were used to worship false gods and the real God; regardless, the worship at the wrong location was a sin and a mark against Joash. It was the mark against another great king, Josiah. Josiah came to power at a time when the people of Judah had lost the Law of the Covenant, but it was found under Josiah's reign. Josiah had the Law read to the people and had them reconsecrate themselves to the Lord. Josiah was a great king, but he didn't remove the high places either. This asterisk was given to several other good kings that did their best to end idol worship and to focus on the real God.

If you were to die today and your eulogy given, what asterisk would mark your life?

The Bible does offer us examples of kings that tore down the high places. Hezekiah was one such king. The commencement of his reign is detailed in 2 Kings 18:

> **[Hezekiah] did what was right in the eyes of the Lord, just as his father David had done. He removed the high places, smashed the sacred stones and cut down the Asherah poles ... Hezekiah trusted in the Lord, the God of Israel. There was no one like him among all kings of Judah, either before him or after him ... And the Lord was with him; he was successful in whatever he undertook.**

Notice the difference between Asa and Hezekiah- both kings were said to have done what was right just like King David did. Yet, Hezekiah was a king unlike any other in Jewish history. The one difference in their reigns was the demolishing of the high places.

The issue of high places is so important because we must understand where worship was supposed to take place: Jerusalem. The location of worship does not seem like a huge deal to Christians because of us having Jesus in our hearts, so everywhere is a legit place to worship; however, the high places have a meaning for us. Mountains were an important part of Jewish lore and history- so much so that God referred to the heights in Ezekiel to give the Remnant hope. Heights and mountains pop up several times throughout the Bible. Moses received the Ten Commandments on Mount Sinai; the Temple of the Lord was on Mount Zion; Jesus was transfigured on Mount Tabor; and there are over 500 mentions of mountains in the Bible. These mentions of mountains illustrate how we should view Ezekiel's words about Mountains of Israel in two main ways: a place to build up our faith and a place to gain instruction.

Think of the holiest, the most spirit filled person, or the most religious person that you know. What is the one thing that makes their faith stronger than yours?

Mt. Sinai is probably the most famous mountain in the Bible; Moses went up to Sinai for days at a time and received instruction from God. Moses would climb Mt. Sinai close to ten times, which was crucial to prepare him for the desert that was to come. We remember Mt. Sinai for Moses bringing down God's instruction for others, the Ten Commandments; however, few people remember that Moses does not get the Ten Commandments until his fourth trek up the mountain and the tablets containing them until the sixth visit. Most of the meetings revolved around Moses going between God and the people to set up a covenant. This required Moses to educate the people on what the covenant meant- instruction was God's focus.

In one of his trips, Moses was also instructed to warn the Israelites that the mountain was a holy place and therefore to be respected, i.e. don't touch it when God's presence was on Sinai. I cannot help reading this voice without thinking of my time as a basketball coach. I used to run a drill called Orange Line-No Touch-Oh; this was a drill that was to teach kids to get the ball out of bounds quickly to start a break. The Oh part came because touching the orange line on the court was a violation and an instant turnover. There are few things more embarrassing than touching the out of bounds line on an inbound. Making this mistake will draw, at best, an "Oh my word" from the coach and jeers from the opponents. For a basketball player, touching the line is a shameful event, but one that happens when players are sped up: it takes teaching and training to protect oneself from this mistake. For the Israelites, failure to treat God's presence with proper respect led to death. God was not a capricious

God that just wanted to randomly kill people, so He taught Moses the rules- this teaching came up on the mountain. God has no desire to see us destroyed, humiliated, or dead (spiritual or physical)- this is the God that sent His Son to die for us on the cross in order to grant eternal life and that raised His friend Lazarus. Still, there are rules that must be followed or natural consequences happen. Thankfully, God gave the Jews and us a book of instruction on how to avoid these natural consequences, which came to us at a mountain top.

Getting instruction from God on the mountain is not confined to Moses. The disciples also received instructions from God when the three closest disciples saw Jesus transfigured on Mt. Tabor. Peter, James, and John had a miraculous interaction where they saw Elijah and Moses meeting with Jesus; this meeting ended with God stating that the disciples were to listen to Jesus. Was this a minor statement? For us it was, but the disciples had a habit of needing extra prodding to actually listen to Jesus's words. The added instructions could have saved Peter from sinking on the sea, James and John from calling down lightning on a stubborn village, or Judas from betraying Jesus for a measly 30 silver coins.

<u>What is one negative event in your life that could have been different by listening to God instead of going off on your own?</u>

Jesus's most famous sermon was the one that he gave on the unknown mountain, which we just refer to as the Sermon on the Mount. Jesus took the Law of Moses and ramped it up. No longer were we to say that murder was wrong, but we were to understand that God saw murder in the heart as bad as the physical act. No longer were we to see adultery as a physical act, but we were to see adultery of the mind as just as bad. No longer were we to follow the letter of The Law, but we were to follow its Spirit. This was a new teaching, and it came from the mountain top.

The prophet Elijah also had a one-on-one experience with God at Mt. Horeb; this interaction showcases another aspect of the mountain top Hedge. After his battle with the prophets of Baal, Elijah fled to Horeb. His experience at Mt. Carmel had to have been one that left Elijah in a very conflicted state. On the plus side, he had just completely humiliated the prophets of Baal and led the slaughter of the priests that had led the Israelites astray, actions that took place after God answered Elijah's prayers in a fashion that was dramatic and public. Despite the success, Elijah's life was threatened by Queen Jezebel, which disheartened him to the point where Elijah prayed for death. A lot of us would probably judge Elijah at this point- seriously, how can you be distraught over a single threat when you just watched God light your sacrifice on fire while Baal's altar was destroyed after failing to be lit.

We have all been in Elijah's predicament. He had just gone to battle and found that the battle was not over, so he needed to recharge. God had Elijah walk to Mt. Horeb to rejuvenate. It is interesting to note that Elijah had to walk for 40 days to get to a place to rest. A place to recharge is not something where one just flops down on the side of the road or on a neighbor's couch; a resting/recharging place requires a separation from normal society/circumstances. So, God took Elijah to a place where he could be recharged. After ascending the mountain, Elijah's experience started with a wind so powerful it tore up rocks, followed by an earthquake, and then fire, but it was a gentle wind that ushered God into the conversation. This conversation saw God give Elijah comfort and then directions on where to go and what to do. After this encounter, Elijah would be prepared to continue his war against apostasy, but the recharge had to happen. We get this recharging on a material level easier than we get it on a spiritual level. All of us have had to set our phone aside to let a dying battery recharge- leaving it alone prepares it for its next use. Trying to use the phone during charging only prolongs the time it takes to fully restore the phone. We are the same way and need to be away for our quiet, recharging time, yet our society rarely takes time to recharge.

As in all things, Jesus is our greatest role model. Think about the times that Jesus preached to people and spent his time helping others. He went away to a private place to pray to God. Jesus understood the need for quiet time, a time for strengthening one's faith. The greatest example of Jesus needing to be recharged was when He went to the Mount of Olives to pray to God for strength for the upcoming crucifixion. Jesus pleaded for another path but ended with "not my will but Your will be done". Jesus left the mountain ready for what He had to do.

All of this mountain talk is interesting, but the question still remains on how this applies to the Hedge. Simple, the Hedge and the mountain are linked together. The mountain is where we go to be safe and focused in God's presence, and we need to be behind our Hedge to be safe and free of distractions. Safety is an important aspect of the Hedge and the mountain because it gives us time to let our guard down and be vulnerable with God. No one gets close to another person until the guard is let down. Healing is not done until the guard is let down. Trust is not built unless people open up and show an inner part. Growing in God requires us to be willing to take off our personal protection and have God look at our innermost being.

Think of the mountain top as our place to go to school; think of school as our place to prepare us for the role that we are to play. One of the greatest complaints about schools today is that the number of shootings has made the halls unsafe to learn. This is a fair statement as learning is really difficult if the learner is not safe. In order for Moses to learn from God, he needed to be safe. God created a Hedge that would shield Moses from the distractions of the world, the complaints of a rebellious people, and the day to day grind of running a nation. It is interesting to note that Moses's face always glowed after these meetings with God, as the mountain for Moses was a time of intimate interaction. It was a place where Elijah was safe from Jezebel. The people were safe from the cares of the physical world while on the mountain with Jesus, remember He was able to feed them with one person's lunch. Learning from and recharging with the Lord happens in a safe spot.

I think pets illustrate this the best. I am a huge cat person. I have two cats that will come up to me, lay down on my chest, and completely let their guard down to the point that they look comatose. It was not always like this though. When my cat Tessie came home with us, she was a very timid cat that would not trust us. She hid inside the furniture and ran away when she saw us. There was no way that she would have laid down on my chest to take a nap. She had her guard up, and it limited my ability to love on her. Now, I will go pick her up, place her on my chest, and pet her into a purring coma. Every person knows enough to avoid picking up a strange cat. My dad tried once with a kitten that he thought was ready to be picked up and cuddled; my dad told me that he did not know that blood could shoot out of a thumb like a water hose. The cat did not feel comfortable letting his guard down and accepting the love that my dad was willing to give. Tessie is willing because she trusts me to keep her safe.

God requires that we let our guard down to fully feel His presence and his love. We have to trust Him to keep us safe. This is where the Hedge comes in- our safe place. Historically, the high ground was seen as the safer place to be, and the same can be said about the Hedge. The key is not safety though. In the Book of Acts, Peter walked right out of the jail and returned to the disciples. God stopped the sun to give the Israelites a victory over the Amorites. The Red Sea demolished the greatest army in the world while letting the Israelites walk by in safety. The issue is not about protection, God can do that in many ways; the issue is one of us having a place to come and get a word, a recharge, and a pat on the back. We must have the place where we worship God. For the Jews, this place was the Mountains of Israel. Today, it is anywhere that is free of distractions.

I must say that the mountains around Yellowstone were beautiful. Actually, all of Yellowstone was beautiful- it was everything that my dad promised me that it would be. It took me to go up the mountain to see it though. Being in the mountains was a near religious experience for me. I got to look at God's amazing creation and feel His peace. I was even able to let my guard down and let my kids experience this masterpiece of creation without fear. This experience changed my view of heights and mountains. I feel the most at peace when I am in the mountains. Now, my wife and I choose to go on vacations where we hike up the mountains. We just took a vacation hiking in the mountains of Glacier National Park, and I drove the winding Going to the Sun Road that hugs the mountains of Glacier.

Despite my new view on the mountains, I do have to confess that I did not go in on the Beartooth Highway. I was not ready for it, but I did go up to the mountain a different way. This trip grew me and prepared me to take a shot at it later in life. At some point, I'll be ready for that chance. Elijah was not ready for all of his mountains at first. His moment with God on the mountain came after his greatest victory: Mt. Carmel. Most people forget that Elijah did not go from his initial calling to Carmel on a direct line. Before Carmel, he spent an undetermined amount of time being fed by ravens. I had a professor in college suggest that this period might have lasted up to three years. Each of us needs a different amount of time in the mountains to prepare us for the battle ahead. Moses went up the mountain several times; Elijah needed one time. I think that Going to the Sun Road in Glacier prepared me to handle Beartooth, but if it hasn't, I will just continue going up mountains until I am ready.

What do you need to do to have a better Hedge?

The Hedge of Fruit

I grew up on a short 40-acre farm that was a hunter's paradise. The 20-acre field had a crop of soybeans every year, and there was 20 acres of forest attached. At this point, you're probably assuming that I was your traditional rural boy that grew up hunting, fishing, and farming. Yeah, I wasn't that interested in any of those activities, but I really loved growing up on the land because of the hedge of trees that circled the roadside of the farm. In particular, I loved two trees the most: two pear trees. I would look forward to harvest time for the chance to pick bushel after bushel of pears. There are few things better in life than a perfectly ripe, freshly picked pear.

Actually, I can immediately come up with something better than those fresh picked pears- my grandmother's canned pears. Her canned pears should be banned, and probably would be today. They sat in a sugary liquid that brought out the flavor of the pear and added in ways that experiencing it might border on sinful. Okay, the canned pears were not a sin, but they were amazing. I haven't had a jar of her canned pears in at least two decades, but I can still remember the taste. I guess the memories of these pears is why I was so excited when I bought a house with a pear tree.

This pear tree illustrates another example of how the Hedge is useful and how it fits in with our previous chapters on the mountain aspect of the Hedge. To really understand how the Hedge interacts with the

Heights and Fruitfulness, we need to go to the main passage where the Hedge is mentioned: Job 1.

> **In the land of Uz there lived a man whose name was Job. This man was blameless and upright; he feared God and shunned evil. He had seven sons and three daughters, and he owned seven thousand sheep, three thousand camels, five hundred yoke of oxen and five hundred donkeys, and had a large number of servants. He was the greatest man among all the people of the East. (verses 1-3 NIV).**

First, let's look at what we know about Job. The guy is wealthy beyond belief. I would say that he is the Bill Gates, the Jeff Bezos, or the Elon Musk of his day, but there was a very huge difference between Job and them: Job was blameless. The next couple of verses would describe how Job would offer sacrifices for his children on the chance that they had done something wrong. He hated evil and did the right thing. Job was the greatest man of the East; I would argue that he would have to be put on the level of Enoch and Elijah, two men who were taken to Heaven without experiencing death.

No man should have questioned Job's integrity, but there was an adversary that did. Verses 6-11 of Chapter 1 describe how the devil thought that he could show that Job's faith was just built on an impenetrable hedge and not a deep-rooted love.

> **One day the angels came to present themselves before the LORD, and Satan also came with them. The LORD said to Satan, "Where have you come from? Satan answered the LORD, "From roaming throughout the earth, going back and forth on it." Then the LORD said to Satan, "Have you**

considered my servant Job? There is no one on earth like him; he is blameless and upright, a man who fears God and shuns evil." Does Job fear God for nothing?" Satan replied. "Have you not put a hedge around him and his household and everything he has? You have blessed the work of his hands, so that his flocks and herds are spread throughout the land. But now stretch out your hand and strike everything he has, and he will surely curse you to your face.

The key to understanding the battle plan is to realize that there are two things that can be attacked: faith and works. James gives us perhaps the most important tenet of our Christian walk in the second chapter of his book: faith without works is dead. Faith requires a tangible result to show that the belief is alive- we call this the work or the fruit. While faith is the key to our relationship, too often we focus on the works as the most important aspect of faith. Many people that fall away from the faith do so because they do not see the answers to their prayers, or they see some bad event in their life. I follow two different prayer chains every day, and I have loosely tracked the subject of the prayer requests. I see about three prayer requests regarding a thing (e.g. new job, healing from a physical illness, or loss of a loved one) to one about the person's faith. Honestly, most faith related prayers are directed at the salvation of a loved one, so taking out the faith of a loved one prayer, the ratio of thing to faith prayers is closer to 9 to 1. There is nothing wrong with praying for a new job, healing, protection of property, or for a loved one's salvation; in fact, we should be praying for these things- we are called to pray for these.

Look at what you say during prayer and give rough estimates of how much of what you say falls into these three categories: prayers for a physical thing (health, job, house, etc), prayers for a faith thing (salvation, growth in hard times, etc), and praise.

<u>Are you happy with these percentages?</u>

<u>What changes can you make to your prayer life today?</u>

The issue with our prayer focus is that it illustrates a path for us to be drawn away. The path that the devil chose to use against Job was the thing. The thing, aka the work, is the outcome of our faith, our calling, and our walk. We believe that God gave us a job or wants us to have a job- true, but too many of us fixate on the job instead of the God that can meet our needs without a job. The disciples made it work without jobs in the early days after Jesus was crucified. Jesus had Peter throw a line into water in order to catch a fish that would have a coin that could be used to pay the Temple tax for Peter and Jesus. Jesus said that God takes care of the sparrows and clothes the grass of the field with flowers to the point that the grass has more splendor than Solomon. God will provide, but we focus on the work because it is tangible instead of an intangible- faith.

The devil knows people, so he will go after the work to get at the faith. Think of Jesus being tempted in the wilderness. Jesus was told to do a miracle by throwing himself down (a physical act to manifest a miracle) in faith that God would send angels to save Him (a physical act done in faith). Jesus was told to use His faith to turn stones into bread (a physical result of faith). Jesus was offered the entire world (a physical possession) if He would switch his faith to another. In each case, the devil tried to sever Jesus's faith by going after a work. For humans, the physical manifestation of faith trumps the unseen act of faith. This is how the devil went after Job.

<u>Where does the enemy attack you the most? Is it a physical thing or your faith?</u>

I have had some bad days in life, but Job really got hit. In a matter of minutes, he was told that his children were killed, his camels were stolen, the donkeys and oxen were stolen, the sheep were killed by a fire from the sky, and the servants were all put to the sword. Most people today and Job's contemporaries would have seen Job's greatness as his wealth. The Bible would say that these things would show God's blessing. Everything points to what Job just lost as being dear and important. The devil was sure that he could use the oldest trick in the book to get what he really wanted: Job's faith and therefore his soul.

Problem with this plan is that extreme faith clings to God during turmoil. True faith manifests itself in a work: complete reliance on God regardless of the circumstances. Hebrews 11 is often called the Faith Chapter or the Faith Hall of Fame. I think that too many of us forget that each Hall of Fame member was credited with righteousness because of the works that displayed the faith. Abel **brought** a better sacrifice, Abraham **took** Isaac up to the mountain, Joseph **planned** his burial, Moses performed the miracles, and Rahab **housed** the spies. Each person's faith was made known by the physical. While it is not in Hebrews 11, Jesus's sacrifice on the cross was the ultimate physical act of faith and obedience.

What physical things do you do to show your faith?

How many of your physical actions would you say are faith inspired or showcase your faith?

Faith requires an action. Think of the Judge Barak who "freed" Israel from Canaanite rule; he lost out on the glory of defeating the Canaanite king because he refused to go to battle unless the prophetess would go with him. His lack of action showcased a lack of faith. King Jehoash of Israel was told to shoot arrows out a window to signify God's attack on the King of Aram, but Jehoash went through the motions and only shot three. His faith was such that he didn't see a work as anything but ceremonial and not a manifestation of that faith. The Bible states that the Israelites were oppressed by the Aram king for Jehoash's entire reign. Judas Iscariot strayed back into his old habits of greed and envy, and his faith was not strong enough to keep him following in Jesus's teachings.

Judas Iscariot illustrates the circular nature of faith and works. Our works show the depth of our faith, and our faith is shown in our works. Our faith must bear fruit. The devil thought that destroying the fruit would break this circular cycle and end Job's faith, but he was wrong. The loss of the fruits of Job's faith and his hedge did not impact the faith as the seeds that God had planted in Job's heart were not touched. This was true for Job, but he was one of the greatest men of all time. You and I aren't at Job's level, so keeping our Hedge strong is important to keep our faith-works cycle intact. Honestly, the Hedge was key for Job as well. The way that he got to be the man that he was built on God's protection to foster the faith that Job wanted to cultivate. We as people have to work to build our faith. The church calls our faith a walk. A walk means two things: we have to be moving forward (growing) and we have to work. These works take us on a journey to our Promised Land- Heaven.

I want to go back to Ezekiel 36:8 to help us draw in faith, works, and the Hedge.

> **But you, O mountains of Israel, you will put forth your branches and bear your fruit for My people Israel; for they will soon come home.**

Remember, Ezekiel was preaching to a people that had just lost their Promised Land. This was a land that was flowing with milk and honey. This flowing with milk and honey is, just like Job's circle of faith and works, more than just the physical. The milk and honey represents God's provision for the faith and obedience given. Every time that the Israelites lost the faith, God allowed the land, the manifestation of faith, to be imperiled. This resulted in the destruction of Jerusalem and the loss of the Promised land- what the Israelites had worked to build. The Israelites worried that the loss of the works would lead to the loss of the calling and the designation of God's Chosen People. Ezekiel was called to tell them that both would be known again.

Still, we look at the coming home as the key to a restoration, but the coming home part is the end game. Coming home is the written last for a reason- it is the least important part. The bearing of fruit comes first, but the bearing of fruit is linked to the seeds of faith; therefore, we must realize that the Promised Land is more than just the manifestation of the faith of following God into the land. The return after fruit is grown shows that the Promised Land was supposed to have a different role. Remember, God removed his hand and let the surrounding kingdoms attack the Israelites, but when the people followed God, He provided solid kings and judges to reaffirm the borders. The Promised Land must be seen as a Hedge where the Israelites could grow their faith and their works until they were ready to go forth.

As Christians, we need a place to prepare and to grow before we have the requisite faith for the manifestation of our faith to coalesce into the visible/tangible work. Think of the Exodus where the Israelites had to wander for 40 years in the desert before they were ready to cross over to take the Promised Land. This was not 40 years to claim possession of a prize: it was preparation to take it by force. The faith of the Israelites was not where it needed to be to win victories. The Israelites started to walk a path of pride after Jericho and were routed by the small town of Ai. The victory was contingent on faithfulness.

The proper timing and preparation of events was also something that Paul realized. In Acts 16, Paul is repeatedly prevented from going to preach in Asia Minor. We are not given a reason in the Bible, but

I would have to surmise that someone was not ready for this event and needed more time to prepare their spiritual soil for the proper harvest. Could it have been the people in Asia Minor who needed the time? Maybe. It could also have been Paul. He was the one that needed to deal with the "thorn in his flesh" to keep him growing. Regardless, a Hedge was put up to keep Paul from leaving his area of planting so that the soil was not seeded prematurely.

The rest of the verse in Ezekiel adds to why the Hedge was so needed to keep the works-faith cycle in proper order. Mountains are not known for being great places to grow food. Mountain dwellers had to be creative with their crops. The Incas dug terraces to plant their crops and would water the top terrace and let the water drain down. They became masters of growing crops, even breeding tomato types that were designed for certain altitudes. They had to be creative with their crops and with their water to find success. Growth required a lot of time, but it required even more set up work.

Perhaps the most interesting modern example of the patience that is required to bear fruit is the 40 Fruit Tree. This is a genetically created tree that I came across on the campus of Syracuse University. This tree provides 40 different types of fruit: peaches, plums, apricots, almonds, cherries, and more. A tree that can produce this many fruits is amazing, but it takes time to prep it for an outcome that is not natural. According to the Smithsonian Institute, it takes nine years for the tree to mature. Nine years is a long time, but it takes us a lifetime to do what we are not naturally inclined to do: live a faith filled life that produces the fruit of good works.

When I visited Syracuse to see the 40 Fruit Tree, I came too early in the growing season and was unable to see it with actual fruit. I did, however, get to see the buds that promised future fruit. All around the tree were signs asking visitors not to touch the tree as it was growing and producing. The tree needed its safe space to bear fruit. We need our space behind the Hedge to prepare ourselves to bear fruit as well.

I no longer live at the house where I grew up. I miss a lot of things about living there, and one of the things that I miss is those pear trees. Picking took time, but the fruit made it worthwhile. We picked enough for ourselves, but we were able to get pears for our family members and friends as well. I guess the trees understood the need to produce an abundant crop. Isaiah illustrated how our crop needs to be just as abundant:

> **In days to come Jacob shall take root,**
> **Israel shall blossom and put forth shoots and fill**
> **the whole world with fruit. (Ch 27:6)**

A good tree produces a ton of fruit, just as a good Christian produces a ton of spiritual fruit. Failure to produce is the sign of a dying faith. A dying faith provides nothing to others, just like the pear tree at my house.

For the first two years, my new pear tree gave a limited crop; unfortunately, the tree stopped producing years ago. Oh, the tree looks healthy and gets leaves every year, but it never produces fruit. Too many Christians today are more like my pear tree (pretending to be faith filled) and less like my pear tree growing up (robust and giving to others).

How fruitful would you say that you are?

What do you need to do to have a better Hedge?

Hedge of Growth

One of my friends came to me and started regaling me with his new hobby: gardening. He bragged about the beautiful, raised bed that he had put in his backyard. He promised me that it was tall enough where rabbits could not get to the plants. He left me with an invite to a massive harvest feast. I was promised tomatoes, peppers, beans, peas, and so much more. We would also have home grown pumpkin pie for dessert.

I will never forget the harvest party. I was treated to a small salad, which consisted only of lettuce. Two green beans were doled out to every plate. We had cookies purchased at the local grocery store. I would have gone home very hungry if it wasn't for the hot dogs that my friend provided. After grace, his words to the table were, "I hope you enjoy the beans- they ended up costing us $100 apiece." I guess his foolproof raised bed was not so rabbit proof after all, and the rabbits ate almost his entire crop.

I will admit that we got a good laugh at the misfortune of this neophyte gardener, but Christians are in danger of the same outcome in our spiritual growth. The Parable of the Sower illustrated that many of the seeds planted died without producing a crop. We have already spent time on this parable, so I won't belabor any points. Still, I want to cover the last bit of the Parable:

> **Still other seeds fell on good soil, where it
> produced a crop—a hundred, sixty or thirty
> times what was sown. Whoever has ears, let them
> hear ... But the seed falling on good soil refers
> to someone who hears the word and understands
> it. This is the one who produces a crop, yielding
> a hundred, sixty or thirty times what was sown.
> Matthew 13:8-9, 23.**

Growth is the last area that we need to cover. Jesus said that the good soil was the person that heard and understood the Word. How do we understand the Word? We can only understand by faith.

I want to hammer this home: the only way to really understand the Word of God is by faith. Paul, in I Corinthians 3:19, tells us that the wisdom of the world is foolish to God. It is. We are not as wise, as smart, or as perceptive as God. Think about how Jesus embarrassed the Pharisees and Sadducees. They tried to come at Jesus in their vast wisdom, but He was so far ahead of learned leaders. No amount of wisdom could trap Jesus. God is just smarter than everyone in the world.

Rate your knowledge of the Bible on a 1-10 scale.

Remember that the devil misquoted Scripture to Jesus. Can you notice when people misquote Scripture?

Paul knew this to be true, so his defense before Rome's procurator and the Jewish king did not rest on his own wisdom.

> **To this day I have had the help that comes from
> God, and so I stand here testifying both to small
> and great, saying nothing but what the prophets
> and Moses said would come to pass: that the**

> **Christ must suffer and that, by being the first to rise from the dead, he would proclaim light both to our people and to the Gentiles." And as he was saying these things in his defense, Festus said with a loud voice, "Paul, you are out of your mind; your great learning is driving you out of your mind." Acts 26: 22-24**

Read Acts 26. You will see what is highlighted above- Paul's defense was Jesus Christ crucified and risen from the dead. He did not use his own words, but it was foolish to the unbelieving Festus. He accused Paul of going mad in an attempt to be highly learned. Festus missed the most important part of Paul's defense: it wasn't about Paul. Everything that Paul was about was God's calling. Paul could be rash and feisty, but no one can ever claim that Paul wanted to be seen as more than God's servant.

Paul's faith allowed him to speak God's word in defense. Job's faith allowed him to grow and prosper.

> **Then Satan answered the LORD and said, "Does Job fear God for no reason? Have you not put a hedge around him and his house and all that he has, on every side? You have blessed the work of his hands, and his possessions have increased in the land. But stretch out your hand and touch all that he has, and he will curse you to your face." Job 1:9-11**

We all know the story. Job refused to curse God.

> **Then Job arose and tore his robe and shaved his head and fell on the ground and worshiped. And he said, "Naked I came from my mother's womb, and naked shall I return. The LORD gave, and the**

Lord has taken away; blessed be the name of the Lord." Job 1:19-20

The devil failed because he assumed that Job would base his faith on his own strength. Job's blessing did not come from the strength of his hands. Job fully understood that everything he had came from God. The guy actually worshiped after losing his children, his crops, his livestock, and his servants.

Remember, Job was human. He wasn't able to handle the devil's attempt to destroy his faith because he had superpowers. Job was able to withstand the spiritual attack because his Hedge of Faith was rock solid. The devil tried to expose a flaw where he could ruin Job's spiritual crop.

Do you ever believe that the heroes of the Bible are somehow greater than you?

Where is an area of your faith that is as strong as a Bible hero (Don't tell me that you don't have an area. You're reading this devotion, so you're obviously devoted to God)

We have to realize that Job's faith was the product of that good seed that had fallen on a heart that understood and believed in the Word. Our belief in God, or our faith, is referred to as our fruit. Think about the Fruits of the Spirit: peace, love, joy, faith, forbearance, kindness, goodness, self-control, and gentleness. Think about Job's reaction to a pain that few have ever experienced. Did he have peace? Yes. Faith? Yes. Forbearance? Double check. Self-control? Sure did.

How do you get these fruits? It takes work.

And so, from the day we heard, we have not ceased to pray for you, asking that you may

be filled with the knowledge of his will in all spiritual wisdom and understanding, so as to walk in a manner worthy of the Lord, fully pleasing to him: bearing fruit in every good work and increasing in the knowledge of God; being strengthened with all power, according to his glorious might, for all endurance and patience with joy. Colossians 1:9-11

In order to fight off attacks, our faith must be centered on the knowledge of the Word. When Job's wife told him to curse God, Job responded in a way that follows Biblical teaching. Job understood that bad things happen in a fallen world, but God is in control. We might face, actually we will face, hardship, but hardship is not a reason to lose our faith. Our hardship is a reason to cling to our faith like our very soul depends on it- because it does.

I recently went through an event that nearly shattered me. I came across a Biblical promise in Isaiah 43:2-3:

When you pass through the waters, I will be with you; and through the rivers, they shall not overwhelm you; when you walk through fire you shall not be burned, and the flame shall not consume you. For I am the LORD your God,

This was true for me: I was not overwhelmed or burned. This was true for Job, for Daniel in the Lion's Den, for Shadrach and company in the Fiery Furnace, for the Israelites at the Red Sea, and every person that faces the best that the enemy has to offer and defiantly yells, "Get behind me satan. I belong to the King of Kings, and the Lord of Lords. He has already defeated you. I am the child of the King, and my future is way more secure than yours."

We are going to pass through the waters, through the rivers, and through the fire. Life is not easy, but we have help. You can get through hard times without losing your faith, but you can only accomplish this if your faith is rock solid. Many people experience hard times and fall away. The first attack that we will face will be upon accepting Jesus into our heart. The enemy is going to strike. The Parable of the Sower shows us that belief in God's word is enough to get by this first attack, but there will be more attacks.

A simple belief is not enough though. We are called to mature as Christians:

> **Like newborn babies, crave pure spiritual milk, so that by it you may grow up in your salvation, (I Peter 2:2) Therefore let us move beyond the elementary teachings about Christ and be taken forward to maturity, not laying again the foundation of repentance from acts that lead to death, and of faith in God. (Hebrews 6:1)**

The pure spiritual milk is the belief in God's word, but the post elementary teachings take a deeper faith to understand. Festus could not get his head around an idea that many stumble on- the Resurrection. The Resurrection of Jesus would be foolish without faith, but faith must have works. Scholars have put in the time to show that this event can be scientifically viable. Scholars have put the time to verify that Biblical archeology is accurate. Theologians have created devotions to deepen our understanding. Pastors challenge our faith. Musicians create songs to uplift our spirit. All of these resources are available to help us grow in spiritual maturity. Still, growth is not easy when we are attacked.

I have another friend that got into gardening. He was successful in overcoming the rabbits. He created garden beds on wheels, and each night, he would bring the beds into the garage. Animals could not get to the crops while he rested, and he was able to protect his plants when he was awake. We all have times when we are spiritually recharging; our Hedge is the garage which gives us our ability to let our faith grow. Job was not born ready to lose everything, but he was ready when it happened. Why? As the devil said, Job had a Hedge.

The devil still did not understand though. He just thought that the Hedge allowed Job to grow in materials, but our Hedge is called to grow in the spirit. We are called to pray, to read, to sing, and to deepen our faith. We are called to be soldiers of Christ. God has given us Spiritual Armor (Ephesians 6:10-18). God has us well equipped for battle.

I want to focus though on one piece of armor: the shield. We are given a shield of FAITH. A shield's purpose is to allow you to hide behind or to hide parts of your body. Our faith is a shield in battle, but soldiers spend very little time in actual battle. Most of their time is spent at base drilling, taking care of their weapons, recovering, resting, and preparing. A base is just a big shield. God has given us our Hedge to accomplish the same thing as a base does for a soldier. The base allows you the time to be a good soldier. The Hedge allows you the time to be a Christian prepared for anything as long as you use that time to grow your faith beyond the elementary seed stage.

What are areas in your life that you know your faith is not where it should be?

Be honest with yourself, what spiritual grade are you in? Are you still in basic elementary school or are you seeking after deeper understandings of the Bible?

Choose some are in your life where you will work to increase your Bible knowledge.

PART III

What the Hedge is Not

The Hedge of Fear

As a history teacher, I have studied a lot about war; war is probably my favorite part of history. It is filled with stories of camaraderie, bravery, and success. It shows us what people can do when they are put into extreme situations. Sometimes, you should go and read the stories of people that won the Medal of Honor. I have spent time going through the stories and found some similarities. First, many Medal of Honor recipients got this posthumously. Second, in almost all cases, the recipient left the safe confines of some protective barrier to put his life in danger. These stories of bravery are important in our discussion because it illustrates how we misuse/misunderstand the Hedge in two ways.

Ernest Eschbach was 24 when he landed on the island of Guadalcanal. This island, as was typical of the fighting in the Pacific Theater of WWII, was the perfect example of the horrors of war. The fighting was intense and never ending, and trauma and death were always seconds away. Ambushes were common and coldly calculated to leave not just a physical scar but a mental one. Eschbach told the Morning Call newspaper about living in a foxhole for weeks, where they would not be able to take care of most of their sanitary needs and were only able to clean their clothes in coffee tins.[5] They lived their lives hiding under tree leaves and feared to leave the foxhole.

---

5   Vendiatta, David. (November, 2002). *Deadly patrols, fearful nights in a foxhole on Guadalcanal* . Morning Call. https://www.mcall.com/2002/11/11/deadly-patrols-fearful-nights-in-a-foxhole-on-guadalcanal/

The foxhole that Eschbach described, a description that reflected every foxhole in every war I have studied, illustrates how too many of us view our Hedge: a place to hunker down in fear. Eschbach and his comrades were instructed to not fire their guns unless absolutely necessary; people living in the foxhole did not want to give up their position, so cowering in hiding was preferable to action. Interesting that soldiers were told not to do the very thing that a soldier is trained to do, but Eschbach's orders are actually followed by so many soldiers even when they are ordered to attack. The historian and WWII expert Slam Marshall interviewed soldiers after battles and came to a startling discovery- soldiers in battle won't fire their weapons.[6] His findings suggested that 85% of soldiers would fail to use their weapons in battle. While the reasoning behind this is debated, it is agreed that fear plays a part in this decision.

<u>What is it that causes you to seize up?</u>

<u>How would you describe your life: hunkering in the foxhole or seeking the Medal of Honor?</u>

In our Christian walk, too many of us see our Hedge as a place to hunker down and avoid notice. Our hedge was never meant to be a place to hide in fear. The Bible states some variant of "do not fear" 365 times. Think about this number for a second. There are 365 days in a year; therefore, we can assume that we were never called to huddle in fear. The greatest men and women of faith put their lives at risk.

> **I have worked much harder, been in prison more frequently, been flogged more severely, and been exposed to death again and again. Five times I**

---

6   Smoler, Fredric. (March, 1989). *The Secret of the Soldiers who didn't Shoot.* American Heritage. https://www.americanheritage.com/secret-soldiers-who-didnt-shoot

received from the Jews the forty lashes minus one. Three times I was beaten with rods, once I was pelted with stones, three times I was shipwrecked, I spent a night and a day in the open sea, I have been constantly on the move. I have been in danger from rivers, in danger from bandits, in danger from my fellow Jews, in danger from Gentiles; in danger in the city, in danger in the country, in danger at sea; and in danger from false believers. I have labored and toiled and have often gone without sleep; I have known hunger and thirst and have often gone without food; I have been cold and naked. 2 Cor 11:23-27

You can say a lot of things about Paul, but no one can ever question his zeal for his faith or his willingness to face danger. The apostle Peter was crucified; John was beheaded; Stephen was stoned; and the author of our faith was flogged, beaten, and crucified. We are not called to cower behind a hedge, in a hole, or in any other location that you can conjure. Remember that Parable of the Talents where the wicked servant buried his talent in the ground. His master was irate and took what little he had and gave it to another. What made the servant wicked and deserving of being cast out? He lived in fear.

We are called to be bold. When Moses sent out twelve spies into the Promised Land, only Joshua and Caleb came back with a favorable report. When asked, the other ten admitted that the land was everything God had promised: flowing with milk and honey; however, the men fixated on the words captured in Numbers 13:28-29:

> **But the people who live there are powerful, and the cities are fortified and very large. Even saw the descendants of Anak there. The Amalekites … Hittites, Jebusites, and Amorites live [there].**

Let's look at what they said with the proper lens. The cities were large and fortified. True, but the Israelites had around 600,000 men. Do you know how many people that really is? Let's put this into perspective. The United States is the third largest country in the world and has over 100,000 registered cities, yet the US only 30 cities that contain more people than Israel had men ages 20 and older. The number in Exodus does not count children and women. I had a professor in college that said he estimated that there were two million people that took part in the exodus. This would put the population of the Israelites only behind New York, Los Angeles, Chicago, and Houston. Did the Promised Land really have cities bigger than New York or LA? Does it matter? The Israelites had numbers, if that mattered.

<u>How often do you look at the "numbers" in your life when deciding what God can or cannot do?</u>

It didn't matter for the Israelites had just witnessed God part the Red Sea, go before them as a pillar of fire, wipe out the Egyptian army, enact the Passover, drop food from the sky every morning, draw water from a rock, and perform hundreds of other miracles. At the time, Egypt was one of the strongest nations in the world, if not the strongest, and God had just totally demoralized Egypt. See the number of people on the enemy side didn't matter because Israel had God. He was more than enough to overcome any nation.

In proper perspective, the Israelites ignored the strength that they possessed and the God that they possessed, but their greatest failure might have been ignoring who they were. You see, the ten spies saw the other nations and how strong they were, but they looked at the sons of Anak and cowered. It is important for us to understand who the Israelites thought that the sons of Anak were. We do know that this group of people were a very tall group. We can speculate just how tall by comparing them to a Goliath, who was over nine feet tall, or we can look at the legend that went with them. Many at that time thought that they were the descendants of the Nephilim. Many of us are probably not super familiar with this term, but we probably remember the story of the "sons of God" coming down and marrying the women of the land (Genesis 6). These "sons of God" were also described as fallen angels that were completely evil and went with the devil when he broke from God. Basically, the Israelites saw a group of men that were, in their mind at least, descendants of superhuman beings, totally bent on evil, and against God in every way.

I have to admit something at this point. I am taller than most people, so I don't look up to many people. Still, I was with my daughter at the Santa Monica pier and was walking next to a guy that, according to my daughter, was at least a foot taller than me. I only came up to this guy's shoulder. He towered over me. He made me, a man who is taller than 98 to 99% of the world, look puny. I have been next to collegiate/NFL lineman that are my height and 100 pounds heavier; they also make me look small. Perhaps I can really understand where the ten were coming from on this. The ten were used to feeling big and bad as they went out behind their pillar of fire and walked between their walls of water, but now they witnessed people that were bigger and had supernatural help. Yes, they might have had relation to angels and were bigger, but the ten missed the most relevant point of the legend of Anak and Nephilim: they had been removed from Heaven.

Caleb and Joshua had a better understanding of the situation. The reason that the fallen angels and the devil left Heaven is that they weren't strong enough to take Heaven from God. God was stronger, God was bigger, and God had a track record of winning. Centuries later, Teddy Roosevelt uttered one of the greatest quotes of all time, one which fits the story of the 12 spies:

> **The credit belongs to the man who is actually in the arena, whose face is marred by dust and sweat and blood; who strives valiantly ... who**

does actually strive to do the deeds; who spends himself in a worthy cause; who at the best knows in the end the triumph of high achievement, and who at the worst, if he fails, at least fails while daring greatly, so that his place shall never be with those cold and timid souls who neither know victory nor defeat.

Caleb and Joshua were willing to strive greatly and to disdain fear. This is the faith that the Israelites saw come to fruition when the walls of Jericho came down, showing that these immense fortifications meant nothing. It was the faith that David would show in defeating the giant Goliath. It was the faith that saw Jehosophat defeat three armies with his praise band. It was not the outcome of the ten that were those cold souls that were afraid to leave their hedge of protection and cross the Jordan River. They never got to see the victory despite knowing that victory would come after they died.

The greatest rewards come to those that are willing to take the greatest risk. Our willingness to risk is based on two things: our faith and our commitment. Medal of Honor winners have faith that they are fighting for a cause that is greater than they are. They are willing to pay any price to get the job done. They are willing to go where no one else will go because they want the end prize. For the Israelites, the end prize was the Promised Land, for soldiers it's peace and victory.

Often for soldiers, the price that they are willing to pay is for their friends. Ernest Eschbach noted that one of the greatest things about the foxhole was that it created a companionship that was unobtainable in normal situations. Living a life where you were putting your very life in the hands of your hole-mates built a love and a closeness for which people are willing to run into the teeth of death. Jesus put it best in John 15:13 when he said, "No greater love has anyone than to lay down one's life for one's friends."

The willingness to give one's life is our very calling. We are called to be imitators of Christ, and Christ made the ultimate show of love by giving his life to save us from our sins. Jesus also gave us the Great Commission to go out and save others. How can we save others if we are hiding in the foxhole? Our mission is to be willing to leave the foxhole and save our fellow man. We are called to risk shipwrecks, floggings, stonings, beatings, rejection, ostracization, and humiliation for the sake of Christ.

Is this type of risk easy? By no means. It is made harder by the lackluster faith of our world today. It was easier to be outspoken for God when skipping church could get you fined and when the government officially supported a church. Then again, it was harder to speak out against the abuses that occurred during this time (think Martin Luther). Paul said that it is our weakness that makes us strong because our weakness is what makes us cling so tightly to God- God must be our strength.

One of my favorite stories from the Vietnam War is one that would make Joshua and Caleb proud. Gordon Yntema was the second Medal of Honor Winner from Michigan in the Vietnam War. He was surrounded by communist forces and had just run out of bullets. The vastly superior forces, in both numbers and weapons, closed around him, with guns pointed, and ordered him to surrender. Yntema turned his gun around and started beating his would-be captors with the butt of the rifle. The communist soldiers were forced to kill Yntema when they realized that he would not stop fighting. Joshua and Caleb never looked at the odds, the numbers, the size, or any other excuse to quit. Yntema gave his life to fight for freedom and for his country; Caleb and Joshua were willing to give theirs in faith that they were following God's will. Caleb and Joshua lived to see victory, just like most of us will live through our trials. Regardless, we cannot cower in the foxhole and be afraid to leave or to shoot our guns. We are called to be and equipped to be warriors of Christ. Warriors are only warriors if they get into the fight. Missionaries are only missionaries if they leave the couch. Christians are only Christians when they put feet to their faith, which cannot happen with a life spent behind the hedge. Or, we can be one of the ten that had no faith in God.

What situations in your life do you need to disregard the numbers?

What do you need to hold onto to have the courage to fight your giants?

The Hedge as a Castle

A while back, I went to visit my son who was studying abroad in Scotland. He asked if we could go tour London while I was there and, if so, could we see Buckingham Palace and the Tower of London. As a huge sci-fi-fantasy reader, I have always been captivated by medieval society with its castles, knights, and sword fights. I jumped at the chance to see two of the most famous castles in England, if not the world.

If you have never been to either place, I'll try to explain the difference between the two. The Tower of London is the traditional old school castle. It has the high walls, the guard towers, and an inner citadel that could be protected if the outer walls were breached. The Tower of London is a stronghold that used to have a moat (it is now all lawn) and was designed to withstand the most brutal of attacks. Buckingham Palace is an opulent castle that speaks of wealth, prestige, and elite living. While the two castles are very different in function, they both illustrate a way that we try to view our Hedge and how we try to use the Hedge in ways that it was never meant to be used.

I started this study after watching a Tim Hawkins video where he gave his thoughts on the Hedge of Protection. Granted, Tim Hawkins is a comedian, and his job is to make light of situations and ideas. In the skit, Tim talks about how someone came up to him and said that they were praying for a hedge of protection around him. Tim's response is classic to what some many of us think:

> **Not to complain, but is that the best that you can do? How about a thick cement wall with razor wire on top of that bad boy. A hedge of protection? A good set of clippers would go right through that thing. I'm guessing that the devil has a set of clippers.**

Tim's satirical take on the hedge brings us to an important point, why does God protect us with a Hedge? In the book of Job, the devil states that God put a Hedge around Job and his family. Walled cities existed during this time, so the use of a Hedge was purposeful. See, God does not want us to have a castle for protection. Castles are counterproductive in the very way that the Tower of London and Buckingham Palace are lacking.

The Tower of London is the stronghold that is meant to withstand sieges, attacks, and riots. The moat makes getting to the walls difficult; the walls make getting to the defenders impossible; and the inner defenses leave a weakened, exhausted army with another insurmountable task. The stronghold castle is a defensive masterpiece that assures those living in it have peace and security, which is the problem.

The people of Jericho were in a bad situation. We read in Numbers 2:24 that Joshua had sent men to do recon in the area of Shittim, which included Jericho. The spies came back and told Joshua that the people of the area were "melting in fear of the Israelites". Numbers 5:1 sheds even more light on this:

> **Now when all the Amorite kings west of the Jordan and all the Canaanite kings along the**

coast heard how the LORD had dried up the Jordan before the Israelites until they had crossed over, their hearts melted in fear and they no longer had the courage to face the Israelites.

Rahab the prostitute admitted that she knew that Jericho was being given into the Israelites" hands. Oddly, the leaders of Jericho didn't invite Joshua to parlay a peace talk; the leaders didn't evacuate the city of women and children. The leaders made a decision to hunker down behind their strong walls and wait it out.

The Bible does not give us a ton of what the citizens of Jericho thought- I guess it was hard to get their opinions with them being wiped out and all. Still, I kind of the like the Veggie Tale version of events in Josh and the Big Wall where the Israelites were taunted by two French Peas with one of the greatest Veggie Tales songs of all time:

> **Keep walking, but you won't be knocking down our wall**
> **Keep walking, but she isn't going to fall**
> **It's plain to see that your brain is very small**
> **If you think walking will be knocking down our wall**

I have no idea if the Israelites were taunted, but I do have to assume that the people of Jericho's courage grew every day when all the Israelites just walked around the wall and never attacked. The plan was foolish and ostensibly showed that the wall was so fearsome that this vast army was unwilling to attack.

Pride is a dangerous thing. It leads to us making decisions that are not helpful or are downright destructive. There were really two ways of taking down a castle/walled city: you could attack, or you could starve them out. Armies created a bunch of weapons to attack the walls: battering rams, catapults, towers, and many more. The Israelites did not bring these up the front; instead, they marched around the city with the Ark of the Covenant. We must imagine that the citizens of Jericho assumed that the Israelites were going to try one of the most common tactics to defeat a walled city/fortification: the siege. The siege seemed to be Israel's tactic. Sieges could last months and only ended when the city was so starved that the army was forced to come out and attack.

Regardless of the method employed, the best strategy for those behind the wall was to wait it out. Either the attacking army could be repelled by the wall, or the attacking army might just run out of food and leave. Hiding behind the wall was the strategy and was the one employed by Jericho's leaders. Numbers 6:1 says that the "gates were barred because of the Israelites. No one went in or out".

Here is the problem with this tactic, the same one that we saw in the foxhole: we are not called to be timid. God gave us spiritual armor for a reason: to be in the fight. Paul mentioned that we have a sword; the sword is a weapon that requires close combat to be useful. Our Hedge was not made to be invincible because we aren't supposed to hide behind a wall of fear or false protection.

We are called to move. I have always loved the song "I have decided to follow Jesus". I came to Jesus in high school, but I still see myself as growing up with this song. I admit though I never sing it anymore; well, I don't sing it in English. I studied in Quebec to learn French, and I have adopted the French version because it hits on the very point that I am addressing here: we are not called to be stationary. We are not called to cower in abject fear in a foxhole waiting for death; we are not called to hide behind a thick cement wall in false security. We are called to go forth. Let's look at the two different versions of the song.

The English Version
I have decided to follow Jesus
I have decided to follow Jesus
No turning back, no turning back

The French Version
J'ai decide de suivre Jesu (I have decided to
follow Jesus)
J'ai decide de suivre Jesu (I have decided to
follow Jesus)
Je le suivrais, Je le suivrais (I will follow Him, I
will follow Him)

The difference in the final line is subtle but important. The English version is the castle version: I'll dig in and not turn back. Is this a bad thing? Not really. We must have tenacity and to be willing to stick with God forever. I like the sentiment in the English version, but I love the message in the French version. I will follow Him. This is active and aggressive; it is a living faith, not a stagnant faith. Progress and growth only happen with movement forward.

Jesus said that our faith was to be like a city on a hill and that no one lights a lamp to hide it under a shade. Our light is called to go forth. Jesus asked what good salt was if it was no longer salty. Our faith was never meant to be hidden behind walls for that faith is good for nothing but to be thrown out and trampled. Faith must be seen. Think of the story of David and Goliath. Saul and the army were camped across from the Philistine army and ran in terror every time Goliath challenged them. The Lord's anointed literally hid behind rocks in fear. The wicked servant buried his talent in the ground. Moses complained bitterly about being inadequate and did his best to get out of liberating God's people.

Gideon was found by the angel of the Lord hiding in a winepress. He was so afraid of the neighboring peoples that he tried to thresh his grain, threshing requires air flow, in an enclosed area. Why would he do something that was so ineffective? He was scared and felt secure behind a wall that could shield him from sight. He hid his actions of destroying the altar of baal by doing it in the dark. He required multiple signs before he would act.

Still, we must give it up to Gideon because he did act. Sure, he took down the altar at night, but his story didn't end there. He would go on to attack the enemies of God after dismissing most of his army. David did not let the size of the enemy dissuade him from addressing a man who insulted his god. While the king and his army hid behind a rock, David defeated the giant with a rock. The key thing is that he ran out.

David was not alone in running out against overwhelming odds. David's best friend was Saul's son Jonathan, who had his own story of heroism. In 1 Samuel 13 and 14, the Israelites were in a bad spot. The Philistines had made it so that the Israelites could not possess anything that could be used as a weapon. They had so utterly defeated the people's ability to fight that the people hid and gave in to the demands. Still, Jonathan had extreme faith:

> **Come on now, let's go across to these uncircumcised pagans. Maybe GOD will work for us. There's no rule that says GOD can only deliver by using a big army. No one can stop GOD from saving when he sets his mind to it**

Notice that Jonathan started with "let's go". He didn't say that they should spend time waiting it out or that they should form a committee or any such nonsense. He said, "let's go". So, he went up the mountain, and the Philistines taunted him by saying "The Hebrews are crawling out of their holes ... come up here and we will show you a thing or two." So, Jonathan went up and killed 20

Philistines. Verses 20-23 of Chapter 14 tell what happened when Saul and the army learned of Jonathan's actions:

> **Saul immediately called his army together and they went straight to the battle. When they got there they found total confusion—Philistines swinging their swords wildly, killing each other. Hebrews who had earlier defected to the Philistine camp came back. They now wanted to be with Israel under Saul and Jonathan. Not only that, but when all the Israelites who had been hiding out in the backwoods of Ephraim heard that the Philistines were running for their lives, they came out and joined the chase. God saved Israel! What a day!**

Notice what happens when someone leaves the protection of their hedge. First, Jonathan sowed fear in the opposing army. Second, people that had defected from God came back. Third, people left their hiding and joined the movement. The passage ends perfectly with "What a day!"

Look at King Jehoshaphat and his reaction to being attacked by Moabites, Ammonites, and Meunites in 2 Chronicles 20. I recently came across verse 12 of this story when going through a very rough situation, and it helped me greatly:

> **Our God, will you not judge them? For we have no power to face this vast army that is attacking us. We do not know what to do, but our eyes are on you.**

I don't know what to do, but my eyes are on you. This is faith, and Jehoshaphat's next step of faith was to leave the walls of Jerusalem.

He told the army to be prepared to attack and then came up with what on paper is the most peculiar military strategy in history: he sent singers to lead the attack. Still, the wisdom of God is foolishness to the world and just happens to be the very thing that wins us the day. The armies of the enemy were put into disarray and were soundly defeated as the Israelites sang songs of praise.

In another chapter, I mention that we misuse the Hedge of Protection in two ways. In that chapter I discussed how we become paralyzed in fear. Here I assert that we can also hide in false pride. Castles and fortresses were a matter of pride. Only a few were allowed into the castle. It was a way of saying that the people that lived there were more important than those not worthy enough to be allowed inside. While the Tower of London definitely fits this mindset, the Buckingham Palace illustrates the dangers of pride in our Hedge to a greater degree and will be the subject of our next chapter. Still, I want to stress that seeing our Hedge as a Tower of London, a rock-solid wall of protection, is showing a faith in self. When I leave, I show faith in God to keep me safe. Saul had faith that the rocks would keep him safe; David had faith that the rocks would solve the problem. You must decide which hedge you want. Do you want a hedge of you or a Hedge of God?

What areas in your life do you have false hope or put more hope in than you should?

What is something that you have felt that you should do but were afraid to do it?

Where is God calling you to go today?

The Hedge as a Christmas Tree Ornament

I was on the phone with my mother-in-law today, and we were talking about these devotions that I am writing. She told me that she was driving by a corner lot on the road and noticed that the owners had placed a hedge around their property. This hedge was a rock hedge that stood about a foot tall. Being a corner lot, she hypothesized that the owners had a lot of people cut through their corner lot and wanted to keep unwanted walkers off the grass or that they wanted to keep dogs from doing their business on the lawn.

The story reminded me of my senior year in high school when I met with a Marine recruiter. I had kicked the idea around for years and thought it would be an honorable career. I stood about 6'4, played three sports my senior year, graduated in the Top 10 of my class (in a class of under 70 but it was still Top 10), and willingly walked into the recruiting office. On the surface, the high school me was the poster child for what a Marine should be. I would have looked great in uniform and would have looked amazing walking into a school to recruit future soldiers.

Looks are deceiving, though. I would have made a horrible soldier. My physical appearance was only half of what I was. I am a person that is a sensitive soul and that lives to build others up; honestly, I do not even like guns and have not fired one in over 30 years. I am also still working on my fight or flight response; I tend to emotionally run when faced with attacks on my character or to my person. Soldiers serve an invaluable role in society; the reason that I can write this devotional and that I don't have to worry that some evil will befall me is that good men and women have spent their lives protecting my freedoms. To protect freedoms, soldiers are people that have to be willing to run to the fight. While not all soldiers use guns daily, being competent with a weapon is kind of a requirement.

<u>What expectations or stereotypes do people have of you?</u>

<u>How do you feel when you don't meet those expectations?</u>

Putting me in a uniform would be ornamental as I am not really wired to do the job. My student knew that I was too sensitive to survive what a soldier had to do; honestly, I'm not even tough enough to be a soldier. Just like a physical appearance can be ornamental, the Hedge can also be ornamental. The Hedge that my mother-in-law saw was ornamental. Yes, the hedge served a purpose to keep dogs from defiling the lawn and protecting the all-important grass lawn, but the Hedge is supposed to provide us protection, safety, peace, and privacy. Just like my height and accomplishments can only make me a Marine on the surface, the Hedge must be more than an ornament that looks good but serves little purpose.

Too many of us, though, are fine with an ornamental faith that protects us just enough for a sense of security. We are safe from minor inconveniences like a pooping dog or an annoying neighbor, but we aren't ready for major calamity. Fences and hedges in the physical world can be expensive to create. They take time. A small little barrier is cheaper and quicker. Many people are willing to settle for the ornamental because it makes them feel good without costing them much.

When I think of ornamental faith, I can't help but think of two Bible characters: Samson and Judas Iscariot. The story of Samson is one of the saddest stories in the Bible. Can you think of someone more blessed than Samson? He was set apart from birth to be a special man, one totally devoted to God. His birth was miraculous as his mother was barren and living in a time when the Philistines had been terrorizing the Israelites for 40 years. His father was a God-fearing man who responded to his wife's news that an angel had told her that she would give birth by asking God for the wisdom on how to raise the child properly. The words of the angel were clear: Samson was to live a life that followed specific guidelines that would keep him pure and would show him to be different from his fellow Israelites.

Samon's life was blessed with amazing strength and, more importantly, an amazing calling. Samson was called to free his people from the yoke of Philistines bondage. His strength was unquestionable and in full display when he went to get his wife. A lion attacked him while Samson was alone, and Samson killed the lion with his bare hands. I think everyone has read this story and come away realizing how cool this is, but we stop short of really understanding how impressive this feat really is. A lion has a bite that is 6.5 times stronger than a human, can lift loads 10 times what a man can lift, and has a paw strength that can hit up to 100 times harder than that of a human. Lions are bred to be killing machines. Samson took on a killing machine that would easily kill even the strongest man in the world, yet the Bible states that Samson treated it like it was a baby goat.

I make such a big deal about this story because Samson was blessed with a life that few ever get to see: he had parents that were totally devoted to raising him properly, he went through a strict regimen to keep him holy and set apart, and he saw God work in ways that no one had ever seen before. Still, let's look at this lion attack deeper. Samson was on the way to find a Philistine wife, something that was forbidden. The Bible tells us in Judges 14:5 that this movement was from the Lord, but what we are not told is whether Samson knew this. Did the Lord direct Samson to this decision? If so, then why wouldn't Samson inform his parents that this was from God? Did God let Samson go his own way while using his wanderings to bring about God's purpose? These are questions we will never know, but we can get a good guess by Samson's actions after he kills the lion. On a return trip, Samson goes back to the carcass of the lion and sees honey being made inside the dead beast, so Samson does what any of us would do and eats the honey out of a decaying corpse. Okay, I wouldn't do this, and I highly doubt you would either. First, I don't like being stung, so I am not going diving into a bee's nest. Second, I don't eat roadkill- neither did the Israelites. The Book of Leviticus had strict kosher laws that forbade eating carrion, so Samson broke a law on his way to break a law. Worse yet, Samson gave some of this unclean food to the very parents that tried to talk him out of marrying an unclean woman and that had zealously guarded their faith and his faith.

Regardless of the reasonings, God used Samson to liberate the Israelites from Philistinian rule. His wedding ended up being a disaster when his wife betrayed his trust by sharing the answer to a riddle, so Samson killed 30 men. Samson destroyed the crops of his wife's town when she was given to another man. The town punished the family by killing the family, so Samson killed many more Philistines. When the Philistine army came to capture Samson, he took a donkey jawbone and killed a thousand men. Samson's exploits were enough to make him a leader and a judge of his tribe for 20 years.

One of the more interesting questions that I have always had about Samson's story deals with the Spirit of the Lord. In the killing of the 30 men and the donkey jawbone, the Bible states that the Spirit of the Lord came on Samson. In the other two stories, no mention of

God is made in these superhuman feats. Did Samson stray outside of God's calling and use his gift on his own terms, or was this from God? I am going to guess, and it is a guess, that some of these actions were on his own. I draw this conclusion from the first three verses of the 16th Chapter of Judges. Samson is seen going into the Philistine town of Gaza to visit a prostitute. While I have no intention to be graphic, I am interested in the prostitute. Where did she work? The use of prostitutes in worship was a common practice in Canaan, and I cannot help but wonder if Samson was visiting a normal prostitute or one specifically associated with a pagan god. What we do know is that soldiers were waiting for him outside the city, so he tore the city gate from the hinges and walked to safety. Regardless of her employer, this visit to the prostitute shows that Samson was able to walk completely outside of God's calling, path, and lifestyle and still make use of his God-given powers.

Well, he was able to walk his own path for a time. Despite having had issues with an untrustworthy wife that betrayed his confidence, Samson jumped into another liaison with the Philistine woman Delilah. We all know the story of how Delilah tried setting Samson up multiple times to be captured, yet he stayed with her. His faith and his calling became so ornamental that Samson's fall was assured.

> **Then [Delilah] called, "Samson, the Philistines are upon you!" He awoke from his sleep and thought, "I'll go out as before and shake myself free." But he did not know that the Lord had left him. Judges 16:30**

The saddest part of the story is that Samson was not even aware that he had lost God. His hair, which was a sign of his devotion to God, was ornamental and no longer a lifestyle. Yes, he had the long hair forever, but he was not living the Nazarite vow of being different. He was no longer walking in the way of the Law. He was a typical

21st Century Christian: devout from 9 to 11 on Sunday morning and walking a separate path the other 166 hours of the week.

Perhaps Judas's story is sadder than Samson's. To show how sad his story is, I have to ask if you know someone named Judas. I know a Samson or two, and ironically, they both turned out to be powerfully built men. Samson has a redeeming quality despite a sad story. Judas has no redeeming quality. The man literally lived side by side with Jesus for three years. He was there for every miracle, and he was there when Jesus completely owned the Pharisees and the Sadducees.

To me, one of the coolest things about Jesus was that he always had an answer for every trap that was placed before him. Countless times, the religious leaders thought that they had Jesus trapped to either anger Rome or the Jewish people. I don't think that I am the only one that is so intrigued by this ability. Yes, our world is one where we love to have a feel-good story; while we love the stories of the sick puppy that gets better or the kid that overcomes cancer, we smile at the story on Facebook and then scroll on to the next story. Now, we do more than scroll on to the next story when we see someone completely get their lunch handed to them, especially when they deserve it. People bought the book "Bushisms" that hammered George W. Bush for his silly comments; we loved the videos that make our current president look as foolish as he really is; and we could go for years on Trump and his small hands. Viral videos come not from what tugs on our heart strings but the ones that make others look bad.

I guess my sin is the same as everyone's sin that we love seeing people get burned. Still, I love that Jesus was the ultimate burn master. Hopefully, you're a better person than I am, but regardless of where you and I are in life, Judas got to enjoy both the cutting tongue and the soft heart of Jesus. Think about this, every day for three years Judas got to enjoy cuddly puppy videos and videos of people getting their just desserts.

Yet, Judas would end up hanging from a tree, from a rope that he tied, and having his intestines spill out of the ground. He did this for 30 silver coins. We can, and should, make a big deal about his greed. In fairness, the guy liked to steal from the collection plate, but I always had an issue with 30 silver coins. It would be like me selling one of my kids for $50,000. In fairness, there were times that I would have traded my kids for a gallon of spoiled milk and walked away feeling that I got the better end of the deal, but those feelings are just in bad moments. I love my kids and wouldn't trade them, but I could understand someone doing it for a billion dollars. I think we would all think that parents selling their kid would be bad, but let's be honest, it's a billion dollars.

This decision was not a spur of the moment decision on Judas's part, and it was not for a sum that was like "wow, it's ten talents of gold". He got chump change, in my opinion. But this is what happens when our faith is more ornamental than it is functional. We are willing to trade something of limited value for something of huge value. I guess it is like my Christmas tree. I love having it up for the month that we have it up. I have a set of four bulbs that my wife and I bought very early in our marriage. I make sure that I am the one that places these bulbs on the tree, and I put them in a place of prominence. Still, I don't sit all day and look at the bulb; I **might** look at them when I walk into the room.

The other thing about my favorite bulbs is that they are on the tree with a bunch of filler bulbs. We have ones that the kids made. We have ones that people have given us, and these work for now because we don't have anything better. We have a ton of bulbs on the tree that I couldn't care less about. I mean after all, the tree is only up for a month. It's not the biggest deal. Just like our faith is okay to be smooshed around a bunch of other things. It is just something that is hanging around in our life for a limited time. Judas took his relationship with Jesus to be the same way. It was useful, and it was beneficial until a better offer came about.

Our Hedge was never meant to be ornamental. It was never meant to be just tall enough to keep a pesky dog away from us. We were called to build a Hedge that was big enough to keep bad influences out and to protect us from attacks. There are so many ways that we misuse our Hedge, but the one that so many Christians choose today is to make our faith ornamental. When do we challenge our faith? When do we hold our brothers and sisters in Christ accountable? I won't ask when we have been part of a miracle, but I will ask when the last time was that you heard about a miracle and your first thought wasn't one of skepticism.

Samson and Judas both had ornamental hedges. It did not protect Judas from himself and his greed. It did not protect Judas from his disappointment that Jesus was not following his desire for Jesus to overthrow the Roman government. It did not protect Samson from his lust of women and his anger issues. Samson's hair looked good and godly; Judas's friends looked important and godly. Unfortunately, their hearts had wandered outside of the safe zone, and their Hedges were too small and ornamental to stop the wandering.

In the movie The Blind Side, the high school coach told his assistant to have Michael Orr get off the bus first because he could give a good first impression before disappointing on the field for his softness. Having soldiers like me would look good until the fighting starts. Yet, Michael Orr's story did not end in high school. He would go on to become an NFL lineman. He was able to make use of what God had given him. Michael Orr became an example to others that have been looked down upon by others, that have come from extreme poverty, and that have less than ideal home situations. Michael Orr chose to change his life trajectory. Judas could have changed his life trajectory. Samson had so many chances to change. No matter what condition your faith is at this moment, you have the ability to go from ornamental to functional, or even beyond functional.

Maybe a better way to say this is that you must change the height and the depth of your faith. Our Hedge and our faith are so closely tied together that they are inseparable. The Hedge has other components than just our faith, but our faith will drive us to build up the other areas that comprise our Hedge. With training, I could have made a soldier. I might not have been the best, but I could at least have protected our country. Judas might not have become a Peter or a Paul, but he could have made Judas into something more than a derisive term.

<u>What area in your life do you need to change from ornamental into functional?</u>

<u>How ornamental is your faith?</u>

Hedge of Neglect

One day, I was sitting in a Sunday School class with eight other men. One of the men started sharing about his life. He began a story that was about some co-workers. These were men that he had to work around; unfortunately, they were less than stellar influences. My Sunday School compatriot started a self-promotion rant that illustrated to himself that he was a better person than his co-workers. I can still remember his words from ten years ago: "Sure, I swear, but not as much as them. I drink, but not as much as them."

The Sunday School man made a mistake that everyone of us has made- justifying our actions or evaluating our holiness based on those around us. I am not going to write on the sinfulness or the holiness of his swearing or his drinking; I am going to call out his judging himself based on others. We are called to keep God as our ideal. We were not made in the image of our co-workers, our family, our friends, or the people that we dislike. We are made in His image and must strive to follow His example. Yet, we often fail to hit the mark.

Have you ever tried to make yourself feel better about the health of your faith by comparing it to another Christian's actions?

If you answered yes, did you compare yourself to the strongest Christian that you know or one of the Christians that stray the most?

I am guessing that everyone knows who King David is for a dozen reasons, one of which is that I have written about him in this book several times. I am also guessing that most of you are less familiar with or are altogether unfamiliar with Eli. He is a lesser-known figure, but he is inextricably linked with David. Eli was a judge of Israel that would train the prophet and leader Samuel. You might remember that Samuel is the one who would anoint Saul and David as kings. This link is minor compared to a link that is more relevant to this chapter: both David and Eli suffered the same Hedge issue.

For those that are familiar with the Old Testament book of 1 Samuel, you might remember that Eli is not spoken of in glowing terms. Yes, he would train one of the greatest prophets of pre-kingdom Israel. He must have done a good job in training because Samuel is a person that the Bible speaks of in glowing terms- there is nothing negative about him. The closest thing that we can say against Samuel is that he made assumptions that the looks of the man were somehow related to his fitness for kingship (see I Samuel 16 for the story). Still, this is the only strike against Samuel. Eli raised Samuel from the age of a toddler, so he did a phenomenal job and should get a ton of credit.

Sadly, the Bible gives Eli most of the credit for the hardships of Israel and the loss of the Ark of the Covenant. Eli had two sons Phineas and Hophni who did not turn out like Samuel; unfortunately, Phineas and Hophni were the priests in charge of the Ark. The sins of Phineas and Hophni were really bad. They slept with the women who served at the Tent of Meeting. This was beyond bad. I think we can all agree that the priests having unmarried sex is wrong, but this is worse than it first appears. Most of us are not familiar with the Tent of Meeting, so let's go to Exodus 33: 7-11:

> **Now Moses used to take a tent and pitch it**
> **outside the camp some distance away, calling it**
> **the "tent of meeting." Anyone inquiring of the**

LORD would go to the tent of meeting outside the camp. And whenever Moses went out to the tent, all the people rose and stood at the entrances to their tents, watching Moses until he entered the tent. As Moses went into the tent, the pillar of cloud would come down and stay at the entrance, while the LORD spoke with Moses. Whenever the people saw the pillar of cloud standing at the entrance to the tent, they all stood and worshiped, each at the entrance to their tent. The LORD would speak to Moses face to face, as one speaks to a friend. Then Moses would return to the camp, but his young aide Joshua son of Nun did not leave the tent.

Let's unpack these verses a little. The most obvious take away about the Tent of Meeting is that God's presence would come down to the entrance. God chose to come in a pillar of cloud to remind the Israelites of the One that led them out of Egypt, protected them from harm, parted the Red Sea, and was leading them to the Promised Land. This was a reminder to the Israelites that they had the chance to meet with an all-powerful God. Look at the part where Moses would go into the Tent and speak to God as a friend. This is beyond cool to me. This all-powerful God was willing to come down and meet with Moses and talk to him like a friend. This tent was so important that the future leader of the Israelites, Joshua, would not leave the tent. He stood vigil at the Tent to make sure that it was safe and that it was properly maintained. The people would worship God when He came to the tent, but it was so holy that the people were afraid to get too close to the Tent- notice the verse where "they all stood and worshiped, each at the entrance to their tent".

It is important to note that the people did not go near the Tent. Moses called it the Tent of Meeting because he met with God.

You can't have a meeting without being at the meeting, but a select few were allowed to attend this meeting- this was an honor and a responsibility. The Israelites remembered that God met with Moses at Mt. Sinai and that the mountain was holy- only a couple of people were allowed to even touch the mountain. This Tent had similar restrictions and gravitas as the most important mountain in Jewish lore.

At this point, you might have forgotten about Phineas and Hophni. Phineas and Hophni were the two priests that were supposed to be the Moses and Joshua of the Tent of Meeting. They were given the opportunity to meet with God, to talk to Him as a friend, and to protect the Tent. This is a huge responsibility and honor, yet they chose to fornicate with the women who were supposed to be helping keep the Tent holy. Yes, this is bad, but we must look at it even deeper. To a Jew, cleanliness was important. In Jewish culture, cleanliness usually referred to a person's standing with God and that person's ability to take part in worship. Being unclean meant that a Jew could not take part in religious practices. The sons of Eli purposefully made the women unclean by having premarital sex with them and then allowed them to serve at the Tent. This would be like me stealing my friend's car and then picking him up in the car- only a hundred times worse.

You might think that this is the worst of Phineas and Hophni's sins, but it was not. They did not wait for the meat offerings to be fully boiled before taking their share; instead, they would demand the meat raw so that they could eat it the way that they wanted. I am guessing your first thought is that I am putting these sins in the wrong order of vileness, but I assure you that the taking of the meat was worse. Think back to the first murder in the Bible: Cain and Abel. The issue that caused this murder was Cain's flawed offering. God rejected Cain because Cain gave an offering that was not perfect. The Jews had specific requirements for offerings. The offering had to be without defect or blemish. This was to be a perfect specimen. The offering was also supposed to be an animal that was in its prime of life. The quality of the offering was vital. The Bible also set up very exact ways that the offering was to be prepared. Anything less than perfection would disqualify the offering just like Cain was disqualified.

Phineas and Hophni defiled the offering by refusing to allow it to be perfect. This had huge ramifications on the people that were offering a gift to God. Offerings could be made to ask forgiveness for sins. The offering had a cost to the person to balance out their sin, but the two people that were supposed to help mediate between God and man invalidated the offering. The sons of Eli sabotaged the entire system of forgiveness, and they sabotaged every other offering type (thanksgiving, peace, purification, etc). It is one thing to sabotage one's own faith, but it is an even worse sin to lead another astray. These two decided to lead an entire nation astray.

Eli was aware of his sons' evil behavior, and it was his responsibility to purify the system (i.e. have his sons killed). I get Eli's pain. There is no way that I could order the stoning of my kids. God was willing to sacrifice His Son in order to bring purity into worship; Eli was not. Despite these failures, Eli must have done a good job raising Samuel because he turned out to be stellar.

Samuel would eventually meet David and anoint him as king. Remember that David is repeatedly called a man after God's heart. The future kings of Israel would be judged according to David. David was a superhero of the faith. We all know about some of David's bad moments, like Bathsheba, but most of us overlook another one of his mistakes: Absalom.

David had many sons, but two sons made choices that led to extreme pain for the entire nation. David's son Amnon would rape his half-sister Tamar, Absalom's full sister. David did nothing about this act. David allowed his daughter to be raped and sat idle because he did not want to bring death to his son. Absalom had no compunctions about the death of a king's son, so Absalom waited a couple of years and murdered Amnon. Of course, Absalom did what most of us would do if we had just committed a major crime- he left the country.

The story of Absalom can be found 2 Samuel 13-17. Absalom would eventually return to Jerusalem (after three years) and spend two years in the city forbidden to see David. Absalom would force his way back into David's presence and spend the next four years setting up a coup. David would end up fleeing Jerusalem and having to fight a civil war to regain his throne. This is interesting to me that David allowed a situation to go on for 11 years without dealing with it. There wasn't going to be a happy ending to this situation, but David could have prevented a lot of heartache by dealing with the situation when Tamar was raped. The Bible tells us that David did not deal with Amnon's crime (a crime in which Amnon tricked David into playing a part) or console his daughter (Absalom would be the one to take care of her). Doing something would have prevented the loss of a second son.

Our negligence does not just hurt us, but it can have a huge impact on those around us. We all know that the abuses of parents have a profound impact on the children, who often will exhibit the same behaviors later in life. Our negligence can cause marriages to fail, jobs to be lost, and relationships to disintegrate. The negligence of David had an impact on those around him. It is easy for us to see the turmoil of the nation in this, but we fail to remember that one of Absalom's first moves after rebelling was to sleep with David's concubines. This was a normal move during this age. It showed the people that the new king had taken everything, even what was the closest or most intimate to the old king.

Put yourself in the concubines' shoes for a moment. You have been taken against your will to satisfy the king's needs. We call this trafficking today, but it gets worse when you realize that Absalom wanted to prove that he was king, so he slept with the concubines in public. This adds to a new level of embarrassment and heartache for these poor girls. To make matters worse, David will regain the throne and banish the concubines to a forced confinement where they lived the rest of their lives without contact. Our negligence might not create a situation where we traffick people, but our deteriorating faith can cause deep scars in those to whom we are closest.

In both cases, leaders of the Chosen People idly watched the downfall of their country. Eli would watch the Ark of the Covenant be captured by the Philistines. On the day of this great loss, Phineas and Hophni were killed in battle. David lost an extra son and his kingdom for a time. In both cases, the failings of Eli and David were not that they stopped loving God. David was the man after God's heart. Eli loved God:

> **[A soldier] told Eli, "I have just come from the battle line; I fled from it this very day." Eli asked, "What happened, my son?" The man who brought the news replied, "Israel fled before the Philistines, and the army has suffered heavy losses. Also your two sons, Hophni and Phinehas, are dead, and the ark of God has been captured." When he mentioned the ark of God, Eli fell backward off his chair by the side of the gate. His neck was broken and he died. I Samuel 4:16-18**

Notice when Eli died. It was not when he heard of his sons; Eli died when he heard that the Ark of the Covenant had been taken. Eli never stopped loving God. David never stopped loving God.

The sin of both David and Eli was that they were neglectful of dealing with the sins of their sons. I want to key in on the word "neglectful". David and Eli were both leaders. Before Israel got a king, the country was ruled by "judges". A judge and a king are expected to dispense justice. David and Eli failed not because they did not love God nor did they fail because they had disdain for the Law. They refused to do work that would have been hard, so they neglected their duty.

This is where we get to the Hedge. Our Hedge is our protection from sin and from attacks to destroy our faith. Our Hedge requires work to keep it in proper working order. It is a daily chore to keep our faith in working order. Growing up, I lived on a farm and had to take care of the garden. The garden required daily watering, daily weeding, and daily harvesting. The key here is daily. We must be in prayer daily. We must read our Bible daily. We must deal with any bad weeds in our life- daily. David allowed the Tamar rape to go for 11 years without dealing with the problem. Eli tried talking to his sons but never did the weeding necessary to remove the problem.

Failure to keep our Hedge maintained is going to lead to catastrophic consequences. It cost Israel a civil war and the subjugation/exploitation by other countries. It cost the man from my opening story his salvation. It happened over the years. He started exhibiting more and more behaviors that were not godly. He started becoming more vocal about the things that he and his co-workers were doing. He became more outspoken on questioning Biblical teachings. People tried to talk sense into him to no avail. He lost friendships as people wanted no part in his new lifestyle. Now, he lives a life completely counter to what he used to believe.

His fall came from what causes every fall and would be the cause of our fall if we let it: negligence. He chose to condone bad behavior because it was easier than doing the hard work required to get rid of sin in our lives. He let one bad thing after another go until his spiritual garden was worthless. I have been guilty of neglect in my walk with God. I am going to guess that you have as well. No one is immune to this. One of the hardest parts of the Christian walk is to stay on fire. Still, we must realize that our faith requires work every single day. We can let a day or two go, but the work will pile up. A strong Hedge will protect us from the occasional laziness, but our Hedge will live not eternally on its own.

Where have you neglected your faith (Hedge)?

Have your actions caused pain in those around you?

What situations in your life do you need to remedy, TODAY?

What do you need to do to have a better Hedge?

Hedge for Sale or Rent

When I was young, my mother's boyfriend took me for a ride in his 1960s black Corvette. I fell in love with Corvettes and have wanted one for nearly four decades. I have never owned one. I have not even driven one. I just know that I want one. I threaten to buy one all the time. Some might say that owning a Corvette is somewhere between a dream and an obsession for me.

Esau also wanted something; actually, Esau wanted something obsessively. Many of you will remember the stories where the twins Jacob and Esau had some brotherly squabbles. Some were Jacob's fault and some were Esau's.

> **Once when Jacob was cooking stew, Esau came in from the field, and he was exhausted. And Esau said to Jacob, "Let me eat some of that red stew, for I am exhausted!" (Therefore his name was called Edom.) Jacob said, "Sell me your birthright now." Esau said, "I am about to die; of what use is a birthright to me?" Jacob said, "Swear to me now." So he swore to him and sold his birthright to Jacob. Then Jacob gave Esau bread and lentil stew, and he ate and drank and rose and went his way. Thus Esau despised his birthright. Genesis 25:29-34**

This one was on Esau. As the oldest brother, he was entitled to a double share of the inheritance. Since there were only two sons, Esau would get ⅔ of Isaac's fortune. Now, I will probably leave my kids a ten spot, so the extra share of my inheritance is in change, but this was not the case for Esau.

In Genesis 14, Abraham, the father of Isaac, must save his nephew Lot from four kings that had captured Lot during the looting of Sodom and Gomorrah; to save Lot, Abraham called on over 300 "trained men born in his household" (verse 14). Now, the Bible does not tell us what they were trained in specifically, but we must assume that these men were trained to fight. The four kings holding Lot in captivity had just defeated an army fielded by five kings. Abraham was going after a group that was a serious foe, so we assume that he had a group of warriors in his household from which to draw. We also must assume that Abraham had more people in his house that were not trained for war, or the Bible would have said that Abraham had taken his entire house.

On top of having many men at his disposal- which would have required substantial resources to provide for their needs, he had money. Abraham went to his Hittite neighbors to buy a tomb for his wife Sarah (Genesis 23). In verse 3, Abraham's neighbors offer to give him any tomb that he wants without charge because Abraham is "a mighty prince among us". The matter concludes after multiple offers to donate the land when Abraham buys a tomb for 400 shekels. Abraham was easily able to afford this price.

Abraham had to be a wealthy man, and he left his money to Isaac. Isaac was not a man that was willing to live off the work of others:

> **Isaac planted crops in that land and the same year reaped a hundredfold, because the LORD blessed him. The man became rich, and his**

**wealth continued to grow until he became very
wealthy. He had so many flocks and herds and
servants that the Philistines envied him. Genesis
26:12-14.**

Isaac became a Bill Gates, a Jeff Bezos, an Elon Musk, and the vast
majority of this was Esau's for the taking. All Esau had to do was to
be patient. Instead, he got hungry and traded half of his fortune for
a meal of lentil stew and bread.

Have you ever traded an item, a relationship, or an opportunity and
ended up with something worse?

Have you ever been impatient to hear from God?

There is so much unpacking that needs to happen here. Most people
focus on Esau trading his birthright for a meal as a sign of Esau's
immaturity, ungodliness, or greed. All of these are valid foci, but there
is another lesson to learn. First, we start with what everyone can agree
on: Esau was hungry. Yes, Esau was hungry, and man(kind) must
eat. How hungry was Esau though? A better question is how hungry
should he have been for his situation. The Bible tells us that Esau had
come in from the open country, where he was most likely hunting
based on his description as a skilled hunter. We must assume that Esau
had an unlucky hunt and came back empty handed. Was he going to
starve to death though? I would assume not. His father was even more
wealthy than the man that the Hittites referred to as a great prince. It
would be mind boggling if Esau could not have gone to a servant or
to a family member and offered something more in line for a meal.

The Bible states that Esau despised his birthright. It would be easy to
get caught up on the fact that Esau could have found a better deal to
get a meal, but the meal is a key part of the despising. Jacob gave Esau
lentil stew and bread- neither of which comes from hunting. Esau

and Isaac are described as having a taste for wild game (remember that Esau went out and hunted wild game for Isaac before Esau was to receive Isaac's deathbed blessing), yet Esau traded a fortune for a meal that he did not even really like. This shows the depth that Esau was willing to go to feed his worldly desires. Esau had a divine inheritance by being the oldest, but it meant nothing to him.

This choice also meant that Esau had no desire for God's eternal blessing. Esau's grandfather received a promise from God that Abraham would be made into a great nation. Isaac was the inheritor of that promise. Esau should have been the next in line to inherit. Imagine, Esau could have been the forefather of the Messiah. He could have had the Jewish nation named after him. He threw away a chance to be the founder of Judaism and Christianity for a meal that he did not even love.

The Scripture tells us that Esau would be called Edom, which means Red, because of this moment. Most of us completely look over this insignificant looking verse. Names do not mean much to us today. Most of us pick names because they sound cool, we know someone cool with that name, we don't know anyone that we disliked with that name, we saw a TV character with that name, and so forth. I am going to guess that you do not know the meaning of your name. I had to look up the meaning of mine. Jews, however, knew what their names meant because the name was part of the identity, the future, or the past of the individual. Hosea named his child, with the unfaithful Gomer, "not my child". The prophet Isaiah named one of his sons "quick to the plunder, fast to the booty". The prophets often named their children in a way that was supposed to send a message to the Israelites. Jabez, of the Prayer of Jabez fame, has a name that means "pain or sorrow" because his mother had a painful birth.

Esau having his name changed to Edom was important and prophetical. The color red is often used to describe feelings of anger and wrath. The planet Mars was named after the Roman god of war because of its red color. Edom would become an angry man and war would follow him. Israel and the country Edom, whose origins come from Esau, would have conflict for centuries. This did not have to be the case. Edom and Israel should have been allies together, but Esau's anger and Jacob's, which means to supplant or to reach for, deviousness caused a rift that would lead to a civil war in what was meant to be God's people.

<u>Can you think back to a time where you went your own way, and it had disastrous consequences?</u>

<u>Did you know better at the time?</u>

Esau is a tragic figure, but we all have a bit of Esau in us. Esau wanted to satiate his worldly appetites. He traded a God given future for the enjoyment of the moment. I remember when my daughter was younger, and we were trying to teach her about managing her money. We had a rule for our kids that they had to wait a month after seeing a toy before they were allowed to buy it. We told our kids that this would make sure that they did not waste their money on an impulse. We let our daughter break this rule once. She found a motorized, talking stuffed dog at the store and had to have it. We relented and let her buy it that day. She loved that dog for a couple of days. Because it was motorized, the dog was not very cuddly. It required batteries quite often. Within a week, she had lost interest in the toy, but she had dropped half of her savings on it.

We, like Esau, are guilty of the same thing. Too often, we focus on the moment instead of looking at the future. How many marriages would be different if a spouse did not think about how tempting that man or that woman was in that moment? Would the average credit card debt be almost $10,000 per household? Would as many kids be abused based on heat of the moment? Would our government make decisions that hurt the country financially?

Looking to the future and to God keeps us from straying and from a lifetime of pain, or from generational pain. I was out with my daughter's boyfriend one day, and he stopped at a bougie store. He just had to have a $300 wallet that was only $300 because it had a bougie name on it. He whipped out his credit card to buy it, but the card was declined. The credit card company put a hold on the purchase because it seemed fishy. The credit card company acted like our Hedge is supposed to act.

Our Hedge is supposed to keep us from self-impoverishment. Our Hedge keeps us from making decisions that hurt our future. As we leave our place of growth, our place of safety, and our place of healing, we have to have that wall of faith. This wall reminds us that we have a place to be. It could be the wedding ring that reminds us that the girl or guy offering to buy us a drink is momentary and that our vows are eternal. This Hedge could be a budget that reminds us that we need to set aside money for our tithe and our basic needs instead of chasing the iPhone 4,000,000. The Hedge could be a friend that warns us that the decisions that we are making will land us in jail. The Hedge is the Holy Spirit shouting to us that we have a divine calling to head a certain way and that the distractions of this moment will not only lead us astray but will leave us with regrets.

When I was in elementary school, I was part of a study where a small Snickers bar was placed on a table. I could take the small Snickers at any time, or I could wait for the adult to come back with a large Snickers. The researchers were trying to determine if young kids had will power, but I think that they were testing man's ability to hold the promised future sacred or to sell it for momentary pleasure. I wanted to grab the small Snickers, but I was able to withhold my hand by focusing on the future. My future reward was my Hedge- it kept me true to my calling (to enjoy the decadence of milk chocolate, caramel, and peanuts). Esau never built an effective Hedge that could help him remember his future. Esau only thought in the moment, and it cost him his future. He neglected his Hedge to the detriment of generations of his family, to the loss of masses of wealth, and to the disappointment of his earthly and his Heavenly fathers.

Esau is not alone in this short-sighted approach to the Hedge. Before Abraham's wife became Sarah, she was called Sarai. In Hebrew, Sarai means princess and evokes imagery of adoration and devotion, which was awful for her. You see, God told her that He was changing her name to Sarah. Sarah can also mean princess, but it can also mean noblewoman. She was to change her focus from being a little spoiled princess to being a noblewoman. Sarah was a promise to bear a child that would become a great nation with members too numerous to count. Sarai thought that she was too old to have a child. Sarah was promised that God could do this in time. Sarai got tired of waiting; after all, what princess must wait to get her wishes fulfilled.

Sarai decided that Sarai knew better than God, so she told her husband to go sleep with another woman. This boggles my mind. I get that polygamy was a thing in the Bible, but every instance of polygamy that I can remember was tumultuous: think of the prophet Samuel and the grief that his mother got from his father's other wife, think Rachel and Leah, think Solomon and his 1000 women, and so many others. I won't judge the fact that Sarai wanted a child. I would not even judge Abraham for taking another wife. Sarai and Abraham will be judged for leaving their Hedge and taking matters into their own hands. This decision led to Abraham sleeping with a woman that was not his wife, bearing a child with this concubine, and then forcing this child and the concubine into the desert to die.

Do you ever doubt that God will answer your prayers?

Have you ever taken matters into your own hand and helped God get things done?

The sins just seem to stack here. First, let God do God. God's timing is not our timing, but it is the right timing. By trying to force God's hand, Sarai and Abraham bore a son that would become the ancestor of all Islam. Please don't take this comment the wrong way, as it is not a slam on Islam. The birth of Ishmael and the future founding of Islam has created years of fighting between Christians, Muslims, and Jews. All three groups are to be blamed for their share of atrocities, and not one group is clean in this fight. Still, the decision to be impatient led to countless wars and atrocities that should never have occurred. Second, handing her husband over to have a kid was a rejection of the kid that God wanted to give Sarah. Sarai was impatient and decided any kid would be okay as long as she could rip it out of the mother's hands and call it her own. Let this sink in. The plan was to force some poor girl into having sex with a man over 90 in the hopes of a pregnancy that could be stolen from that girl. That decision is kind of messed up and just a shade on the evil side. Sarai just told God that an illegitimate, stolen son today was better than the legitimate blessings of God tomorrow. Third, Sarai was denying the power of God in her life. Sarai thought that both Sarai and Abraham were too old to have a kid, but she still told her husband to sleep with another woman. This is saying, "God, you might work in someone else's life, but You won't/can't work in mine."

We are no different than Sarai and Esau. We are willing to sell future glory for happiness now. Every time we make a decision without prayer, we choose to sacrifice God's promise to always guide us. Every time that we skip prayer and Bible reading, we squander our chance to spend time with the King of Kings and the Creator or the Universe, most likely to spend time watching Facebook videos or playing Solitaire on our phones. Every time we sin, we trade holiness and righteousness for five seconds of pleasure that will leave us emotionally haggard. Each one of us is willing to sell our soul, our inheritance, and our happiness to a prostitute. Yes, it's adultery that we are talking about. We are renting pleasure when happiness is freely given. The Prodigal Son squandered his inheritance by visiting prostitutes because in the moment it was fun, but he was left starving, feeding an unclean animal, and being alone.

We are never called to sell our faith in adulterous worship. We are called to use our Hedge as a reminder that God has something better in store for us. Esau was willing to sell his God given birthright. Sarai was willing to rent out the divine inheritance given to her husband. In the Parable of the Tenants, Jesus tells us the dangers of renting.

> **Listen to another parable: There was a landowner who planted a vineyard. He put a wall around it, dug a winepress in it and built a watchtower. Then he rented the vineyard to some farmers and moved to another place. When the harvest time approached, he sent his servants to the tenants to collect his fruit. Matthew 21:33-34**

Look at the Hedge that was started. It covered a growing area perfectly set up to produce a crop. It was safe with a wall and a watch tower. The renters were given a great opportunity. Be patient, follow the plan, and reap a huge reward. Yet, the tenants grew too bold and impatient. They realized that they could make more money by disregarding the agreement to follow the rules. They felt secure behind their wall and with the watchtower. They decided to go off on their own and take what their straying hearts wanted.

This was incredibly short sighted. They should have realized that this was illegal. They killed servants and eventually the owner's son. They had to know that murder would not go unpunished, but they wanted the promise of the moment. They sold a guarantee of future reward in order to worship themselves. This did not go well. As I mentioned, the Hedge is not meant to be a castle to become overconfident in our security- we must always be on our toes lest we stumble over our own feet. We become too comfortable behind our religion; instead, we must realize that it isn't religion that saves us- we are saved by faith in Jesus.

Recently, I had an acquaintance that owned a 90s Corvette. He offered to let me sit in it. Once I got in, he commented, "I did not think that you would actually fit into it." You see, I am kind of tall, and the car was not made to hold me. I was too big for the dream. Christians should be too big (mature) for the wiles and the promises of the world. When we go into the world, we should feel uncomfortable. We still have to go into the world (in the world but not of the world) to save souls and to be a witness, but we should not feel comfortable. The Tenants felt too comfortable in a place that they were not meant to stay. We were not meant to stay in the world to get fulfillment. We are called to spend time in the Hedge to grow our faith in order to leave the Hedge and share the faith. Esau and the Prodigal Son looked to go into the world and satiate themselves with what the world had to offer without having a Hedge. Sarai tried to go out of the Hedge to make God's plan work her way. The Tenants tried to hunker down in a Hedge of false belief to get worldly rewards. We sin just as much when we rent out our faith to the world. Our Hedge (faith, security, relationship with God) was never meant to be rented or sold.

Be honest with yourself, have you rented or sold your soul for momentary pleasure?

What do you need to do to have a better Hedge?

Final Thoughts

As I studied the Hedge, I became more aware of how important faith is in the spiritual walk. This seems obvious, and you're probably wondering why I needed to write a book to realize this. It is obvious; in fact, it might be the most obvious thing in the world. We must remember though that the devil is always going to attack a person's faith. He tried it with Jesus in the wilderness, and he tried it with Job. He failed with both men because both had a faith that was well entrenched.

This book was an attempt to bring an understanding on how to develop the same well entrenched faith of Jesus and Job. In the Hedge of Growth, I underscored that we have a call to grow spiritually from an infant with a basic faith in God. The Parable of the Sower was important in our study because it showed that an elementary faith is based on believing in the Word of God. This is good, but it will not last the test of time. The devil has a faith in God- it is not a soul saving faith. When Jesus cast out the demon at the Capernaum synagogue, the demon shouted out:

> **Go away! What do you want with us, Jesus of Nazareth? Have you come to destroy us? I know who you are—the Holy One of God! Luke 4:34**

The enemy knows who God is, who Jesus is, and how the Holy Spirit works. This basic belief is not enough. You can know who God is without following Him.

No, a mature faith is the one that handles hardship and temptation like Job and Jesus. When faced with trouble, both answered with Scripture. They had a foundation that was unshakable because the Word of God is unshakable. We don't need to go off on our own to handle cataclysms- actually, going off on our own only makes them worse. Jesus knew Scripture well enough that He could correct it when it was misquoted. Job knew Scripture well enough to apply it to his life.

How does one have this level of faith? Our faith must be firmly rooted. In many places in the Bible, we are compared to plants in that we are to grow. A plant has many stages, but there is one commonality of each phase: a plant is almost always vulnerable to something. We are always vulnerable. God gave us Spiritual Armor to help keep us safe in battle. Security is important, and the Hedge is the place where we are secure.

The first five chapters of this book were designed to show what can destroy our Hedge early in our walk. The Parable of the Sower illustrates that we can be derailed by allowing the worries of the world to choke us down, by planting our faith in a Biblical understanding that is too shallow, and by allowing it to be snatched away by failing to believe in the Bible wholly.

The Parable of the Sower chapters were to show how we can survive this introductory time of faith, but it has an application to our later walk. The TV show *Are You Smarter than a Fifth Grader* was a popular show because people loved to watch adults get schooled by children. The show worked because the producers knew that people forget what they learned in elementary school. Jesus told us to have a childlike faith, so we must always go back to review the basics of our faith.

The middle five chapters were how we can take the next steps in our faith. Job was able to apply Biblical teachings to his Hedge (his faith). He was able to handle situations because he was growing, he could tune out the voices that would lead him astray, he had boundaries to keep him away from sin, and he made sure that he recharged his faith. Job was smarter than a fifth grader because he never forgot the basics, but he also was able to start applying faith to real events. He was basically a college graduate (isn't the role of college supposed to be to teach us how to apply our knowledge to a job).

Jesus was at a doctoral level of faith. He taught people the truth, just like a professor would teach. The thing that really set Jesus apart was that He could school other pundits and educated people. Professors write articles and books to show their peers a new understanding of their field. Jesus brought a new level to our understanding of God's law at the Sermon on the Mount. He schooled the religious leaders that had lost their way. He was not doing this with topics that were so esoteric that only God could understand: He did this with basic teachings. He remodeled what murder meant, what coveting meant, and what love meant. These are all renovations on the Ten Commandments.

The final five chapters of this book were designed so that we can keep from being schooled by false teachings. I remember to a group of Christians arguing over issues that was a controversial topic in social media. The topic was over an issue that was highly important for the church to handle, but the was a contingent that thought that we were being ungodly by discussing these hard issues. In their mind, we were supposed to be silent and not rock boats. I am sorry, but Jesus was a boat rocker. He did not do it to be a Twitter Troll; He did it to school false belief. To some, faith was ornamental and rooted in fear. Faith can almost be like pajamas. Most people won't go into public with their pajamas on, but they will relax around their inner circle. This was her faith: don't show it in public but we can say "praise Jesus" behind closed walls.

Everyone viewed her as a very spiritual person. I fully believe that she loved God. Still, she had the wrong view of what our faith is supposed to be: visibly different from the world's faith. A fully mature Christian is one that knows the basics, has applied it to their situation, and is willing to proclaim truth publicly. The last five chapters are areas where it is easy to fall short of the mark in this maturity.

The Hedge is a multi-tiered organism that protects crops in several ways. Our Hedge should have a faith that is just as diverse as a physical hedge and just as protective. We are called to protect our faith and the faith of those around us. The Hedge is a Hedge of Protection, and it is a Hedge of Belief, of Blessing, of Rest, and of so much more.